Michelle Agdulos

Shine Baby Shine

RECLAIM YOUR SELF-WORTH AND HEAL FROM CO-DEPENDENCY

WWW.GET-KNOWN.CO.UK

For my baby girl, Millie pops.

May you always shine bright!

Dear Catherine,

Shine bright
always.

love

MJpilox.

*She believed that the damage to her mind
and heart was permanent,
Until she met wisdom, who taught her
that no pain or wound is eternal, that
all can be healed, and that love can grow
even in the toughest parts of her being.*

Yung Pueblo

Contents

A Thought

Co-dependency is more common than you think. A study revealed by the Huffington Post claims 59% of people who have been in a co-dependent relationship do not know where to seek help. Well, my darlings, I am here to tell those 59% of people out there that you are not alone and there is support and hope to recover, heal and move on.

If you have recently left a co-dependent or toxic relationship, or feel you are not enough and have been putting other people's needs before your own, and you just want to start to feel good about life, there is a reason why you have picked up my book. Are you ready to make a change within you so that you can learn to relax and have fun? If so, I'm your girl! Using my mindfulness and self-awareness tools will reduce your stress and anxiety levels and level up your energy, making you feel good and helping you to start to get excited about life.

This Book Will

Take you from feeling lost and low to getting back to your happier place.

You will learn to take bite-sized steps from survival mode towards methods that will move you forward so that you can thrive in your life. Recovering from a co-dependent relationship may have left you angry and with low self-esteem, full of anxiety and feelings of uncertainty over what the future holds for you. However, by changing your mindset and slowing down, taking a pause and creating space for you, you can give yourself permission to do more of what you love, making you happier.

Help you develop a mindfulness practice that is manageable and flexible to fit in with your life-style and will boost your energy levels.

We get to start where you are right now. I'll show you how to connect your mind and body through mindfulness exercises. These will give you a moment's break, raising your energy levels. Mindfulness is a powerful tool that can heal and release you from co-dependency and reduce your stress and anxiety. By learning to be present in the moment and viewing your outside world with gratitude, you will begin to feel good and motivated to move on.

You will learn to develop and plan in time for self-awareness exercises that will create balance within your day-to-day life.

Rekindle your relationship with yourself and allow you to rediscover your passions.

You will have fun rediscovering your passions and making yourself a priority. Yes, you'll soon be fulfilling your needs and developing your confidence not just to start your new independent life but to really enjoy it, too. By learning the foundations of self-compassion and self-love, you will start to heal and move forward from the past, feeling more love towards yourself.

The specifics – what is available to you in this book

★ I share my own story and my clients' experiences to show you how even in the darkest circumstances you can break through to a happier mindset.

★ Five-minute guided visualisation meditations in each SHINE module allow you time to feel calm and relaxed away from your hectic life. You get to be curious and not judge your negative thoughts. These meditations can be played at any time or anywhere you plan to take time out for you. You will begin to feel ready to start the day with a happier mindset.

★ Fun mindfulness and self-awareness exercises create a calm and relaxing experience with yourself in the moment. Through self-awareness exercises we start to see ourselves and our view of the world differently, which empowers us and gives us a feeling of acceptance and peace. You get to date yourself and do more of what you love, which makes you feel happier about your life. These exercises will help you rediscover what you love to do and get you out of your comfort zone.

★ Free-flow journal prompts help you find clarity in your thoughts and develop a gratitude mindset. By writing down your thoughts, you will learn the power of your words and how to notice your negative thoughts, as well as create clear intentions to move forward.

You will also have the opportunity to join and sign up to my Shining Sisterhood community, where you get to meet like-minded women who share experiences and support each other's growth, gaining access to free resources so you can develop your mindfulness practice.

How to Use
This Book

Your girlfriend guide from surviving to thriving

This book is your sisterhood guide to taking your first steps from surviving to thriving.

What do I mean by that? Well, babes, it's more about lifting your mood from doing everything and anything to cope, to taking a step back, reorganising and understanding the overwhelming feelings you are going through and then making the right choices to move forward.

Let me ask you now – how are you feeling? Be totally honest with yourself. Are you just exhausted? Are you confused or overwhelmed as to how you can start to feel better? Or are you just wanting to run away to a deserted island, never to be seen or bothered again?

I get it! Sometimes the answers do not come to you when you need them the most– but when you start to use this book as your go-to 'mood changer', you will make mindful steps towards shifting your mindset to one that begins to see and look at your world differently, and with potential. You will start to get the hope that change is possible, and then you will own that change, too – but you will also have the added bonus that you won't feel like you are alone on your journey. We will approach it together, through the shared experiences of other amazing women who have been right where you are today.

Your mindfulness lifestyle starts here

You get to have fun being the boss of your own breath, mind and body.

The exercises in this book will teach and introduce you to a life skill that will impact your wellbeing and your inner growth, and bust out your endorphins. This practice will naturally become a coping mechanism that you can employ anywhere at any time.

A mindfulness practice is a lifestyle that commits to living from a place of enjoying the present, living in the moment, and releasing the past. So why not get started now?

A self-care practice that is flexible for your lifestyle

Making it count and planning in your self-care and mindful activities.

You will have your self-love tracker to keep you on track on your progress, and weekly 10-minute exercises that are manageable for the busiest of schedules. This book will guide you through when it's best in your day or week to action your exercise and will help you identify any support you will need to achieve this.

If you miss a day, there's no worries; pick up where you have left off, and release the pressure from yourself to get it done. Remember, this is your journey and there will be days where it's not possible for you to make progress. What is important is that you honour the commitment you have promised to yourself to heal and grow and start to find a new way of living.

Level up your mindset and see your world differently

A healthy mindset has power, and it is your responsibility to take care of it.

That is the truth! What you think is who you are. Stop and think for a minute about what I mean by that. If you think you are not enough or not worthy, then you will never feel that you are.

I get it! It has become a familiar mindset, but this book is about changing that limiting belief into a mindset of gratitude, hope and possibilities to change.

In each module, you will get to self-reflect, gain some clarity and learn to become self-compassionate, showing kindness towards yourself. You will begin to live more in the present, rather than dwelling in the past and becoming self-aware of your triggers and limiting beliefs. You will begin to feel motivated and inspired to change them.

Assessment

What is your WHY and your INTENTION?

What is your 'Why?' that led you to pick up my book? Make sure you give yourself a moment to think about this, and write it down below:

Now, make this intention the main goal to focus on through your journey with this book.

Recognising how you feel right now and honouring it.

Mark each of the following limiting beliefs below from one to five (with one being the highest and five being the lowest), assessing how you feel/see yourself in this moment:

	Score
Self-worth	
Sense of identity or purpose	
Confidence and trusting your own judgement	
Comparing yourself to others	
Feeling burnout and tiredness	

When grading yourself, you may feel uncomfortable or upset. This is normal and actually very good as you're able to identify it, and it gives you clarity as to what you need to work on. You may have found that all the above elements are high on your list to change and work on, which is OK as you will get to touch base on each limiting belief within this book.

There was a reason you picked up this book, my lovely. Without realising it, you know deep down inside yourself that you deserve to feel loved and have the life you truly want.

When you start with an intention (big or small) as to how you would like to feel, see and be throughout your day, it takes the pressure off it as an end goal. You can see it as a process that feels natural and manageable. This book will guide you to slow down and reflect on your actions and behaviours. There may be things you haven't noticed that are not serving you well.

Resources

Throughout the book, I have provided self-awareness exercises and mindfulness resources, so that you can kick-start your mindfulness practice. This will ensure that your coaching experience with me is an enjoyable and manageable process. You can access other free, fun resources, too, at: **michelleagbulos.com**

There, you will find:

★ A self-love tracker sheet to support, monitor, plan in and motivate your journey

★ Five intentional five- to eight-minute meditations you can play anywhere at any time, whenever you need time out to pause to release anxiety or stress and come back to balance

★ Free-flow weekly journaling prompts from each SHINE module to find clarity in your thoughts and co-dependent behaviour patterns

★ Mindful blogs where I share my experiences and outcomes

★ An opportunity to book a 30-minute exploration session with me and create a bespoke coaching programme to suit your needs.

You can sign up to my Shining Sisterhood community group online, with sessions to empower you and where you can share experiences with other women.

You can also access free social media resources on my:

 Instagram
@michelle_agbulos
@meditate_and_shine

For daily posts on mood boosting and coaching advice.

Facebook
Conscious coach - Michelle Agbulos

Here, you can join up with my community, access recordings of live group sessions and connect with other members of the SHINE squad.

Getting access to the support and information you need couldn't be easier. Just follow the links and start your new journey with confidence and ease.

https://www.michelleagbulos.com/a4planner
https://www.michelleagbulos.com/meditations

I am so excited for you, thinking about what you are going to discover and explore in the coming chapters. You haven't even started, but I am so proud of you already in just giving yourself permission to try to make the change from co-dependency to independence and a clear realisation of your own worth. You are totally worth it, babes, and I will be here every step of the way rooting for you. You are going to smash this! So, today is the day, my lovely. Now you get to work on you, and SHINE.

Hello – Let's Get to Know Each Other

I am:

★ The survivor of a bigamous, co-dependent relationship

★ A single mum to my sassy daughter, Millie

★ Passionate that everyone deserves a second chance to create the life they truly want, and I hope to be the one who will cheer and support you to do it

★ A life coach

★ A professional meditation and mindfulness tutor

★ Creative and a lover of colour, fashion and all things sparkly.

I have:

- ★ Studied for two years with Connected Kids, where I qualified to teach mindfulness to families and kids

- ★ Started up my own coaching practice under my name and Meditate and Shine

- ★ Used mindfulness to help me heal and rebuild my life

- ★ Performed on the West End stage in *Miss Saigon* (I still love to dance, although now not in front of an audience, just my girlfriends; I also love to go to the theatre any chance I get)

- ★ Worked in fashion for many years, where I loved giving women the instant boost of looking and feeling fantastic.

I'd love to meet you, so please connect with me:

Website: **michelleagbulos.com**

Instagram: **michelle_agbulos**

Facebook: **Conscious coach – Michelle Agbulos**

My mission

I wrote this book for the woman who thinks she is not enough, so she can rediscover her light and SHINE!

My mission is to coach and support women so they can develop a self-love relationship to claim back their power, happiness and sparkle after leaving a co-dependent relationship.

With manageable mindfulness and mood-boosting exercises, I will shift your focus towards making yourself a priority and creating the life you want. My SHINE programme will guide you to your first steps towards a self-love journey that is fun, builds your confidence and accepts who you are without judgement.

You are enough, worthy, and limitless in all areas of your life, babes! And I have made it my mission for you to never feel that you're alone. Let's do this together and work towards your fabulous future self and SHINE!

This Book Is For

You if you have recently left a co-dependent or toxic relationship and want to get your life back on track, starting to move on from the past. If you're overwhelmed by life's challenges and don't know how to move forward from the shame of a toxic relationship, I'm here for you. My gift to you is to help you find the courage to take the first steps towards finding fun, love and happiness again, because that's what you deserve.

★ Are you struggling with feelings of guilt, shame and blame from a failed relationship?

★ Does rebuilding your life seem like an overwhelm-ingly huge task?

★ Do you want to stop comparing yourself and your life to others?

★ Does starting out as a single mother scare you?

★ Does it feel impossible to plan any time for yourself?

★ Do you wish to feel beautiful and loved, and find joy in your day?

If you answered yes to all of the above – well, honey, I have your back! I have lived and breathed all of the above and know first-hand how hard it is to find the strength to take the first steps. Therefore, I wrote this book for you. To be that girlfriend who understands where you are right now, wanting to change and feel like yourself again. To rediscover that spark that has been missing for so long, longing and wanting to SHINE!

Chapter 1

Your Journey Back

Meet Hannah, 36, newly divorced full-time working mama with two kids. She left her husband, who emotionally abused her for five years, and is now living her life as a single mother. Her day starts with getting the kids ready for school, already exhausted from working late on a presentation from the night before. The kids are misbehaving and she is screaming at them to hurry up and get themselves into the car. She drops her car keys on the ground, then spills coffee down her newly ironed white top. Just when she is about to get into the car, her phone starts ringing – it's her mother calling for the third time this morning to ask when she is going to see her, as it has been nearly a month since she has spent time with her family.

As usual, the school run is painfully slow, and the traffic is heavy because of roadworks. Hannah is saying to herself, 'Why, today of all days, is everything going wrong? I just need to get through today.'

Feeling flustered after the school drop-off, she rushes into the office to get herself together for her first meeting of the day, which is in five minutes' time. The anxiety begins to build up inside her and she starts to overthink – will her colleagues approve her project? She needs this to work out, as she has gone back to work full-time to earn enough money to make ends meet.

Hannah starts to doubt whether she can pull off a good presentation, as the thought of standing up and speaking in front of others scares the hell out of her. She puts on her best game face (as she has perfected the art of looking like she has it all together) and manages to get through it, but she still feels she could have done better. Her boss then tells her that tomorrow evening the team will need her to stay back late to brainstorm for a new contract. Finding it hard to say no, Hannah says yes, even though she knows it's the same night she promised her girlfriends that they would have a drink to catch up.

The women at Hannah's workplace are much younger than her, and one of them announces she has just got engaged this weekend, which instantly triggers Hannah, as it makes her feel bad about herself that she failed in her own marriage. The question pops up in her head: 'Will I ever meet someone who will love me and accept that I have baggage?' and she dwells on this thought back at her desk, feeling that she is not enough. Feeling a need for attention, Hannah logs on to the dating app she downloaded the other day and starts to type a message to a guy who has pressed 'like' for her, but then quickly changes her mind, talking herself out of it: 'What am I doing? I don't even have time to date!'

Feeling very stressed, with a job list as long as her arm, and having had back-to-back meetings, Hannah only has time to grab a sandwich to eat in the car on the way to pick up the kids from school. Never having the time to connect with the other mothers at the school, she feels that she has nothing in common with them. She smiles and is polite, nods while the other mothers are talking, but really does not engage in the conversations, as she does not feel she has anything interesting to say. All the other mothers seem to have it all together, making motherhood look easy.

After cooking dinner, bathing the kids and putting them to bed, Hannah looks at her phone; there on her screen are endless messages from work, her friends and her family checking up on her. Having not managed to get back to them all day, she throws herself onto the bed thinking: 'More people who want more of my time, and the evening is all I have for myself.'

Having found the energy to respond to her messages, she finally switches the television on and begins to feel very sad and alone. While the TV is on, Hannah is not really watching it and begins to scroll through Instagram on her phone. Everyone looks so perfect in their lives, looking beautiful and happy. She reflects on herself, feeling unattractive and comparing her life with those of her friends. Before she realises it, she has been scrolling for over an hour, as it has become a way of numbing out the negative voice in her head. The fear and the uncertainty of what her future will look like takes a toll over her and she begins to cry. Scarred from her past relationship, the pain she holds has become a familiar voice in her head: 'Why did this happen to me? And how do I get rid of this pain?'

For so long, Hannah has pushed her needs aside to please another, not receiving the love she fully deserves. She knows that this needs to change and she wants to move forward, but she feels it's too much energy to face, as she has so little time. When she turns in for the night, it's just herself facing a wall of silence. Hannah lays her head back on the pillow, dreading that she has to get up again tomorrow to do it all over again. Deep down inside, Hannah ultimately wants to feel loved, but she doubts she really knows what love is, and in her present mindset, it seems impossible to find any hope for the future.

Learn to love yourself again

Can you relate to Hannah's typical day? I know I can. Venturing out on your own as a newly single mother, with responsibilities that have doubled up and become financially straining, makes you feel low in energy with no motivation to face it. It feels like you're on a constant emotional rollercoaster each day, leading you to burnout, stress and not finding the time for yourself, feeling unlovable and looking at your body unkindly. Doing everything and anything not to stop and feel what is really going on with you; letting the trauma control your emotions, habits and behaviour, allowing it to get the better of you. Yes, I get it – it is hard, but you are so brave to pick up my book and take your first steps towards choosing *you*! You are not alone. If this is the only part of the book you remember, then remember that you are not alone. Believe me, that feeling is more common than you think.

Over 40 million women in the US have suffered from being in a co-dependent relationship, and more all over the world. It does not matter what nationality, race or job you have, or whether you are a parent; so many people have experienced this. You could be the most beautiful, intelligent woman in the world and still have found yourself having to give up your needs for another. I have coached women who looked like they had the perfect life and sounded like they had it all together, only to discover the lack of confidence and the low self-esteem they had been living with, holding on for so many years while wanting to feel free from their pain.

A toxic relationship does not happen overnight. It is a long-term effect of manipulating the mind into believing that you are not enough, having to prove your worth while your own needs are not being met. It slowly conditions you into a negative mindset where you experience such intense love that blinds you to wanting and needing more. All the red flags were there staring at you right in the face, but within your subconscious you chose to ignore them, which then led you to feel so much shame and anger towards yourself, thinking it was OK, not wanting it to feel real – just like Hannah.

Hannah is repeatedly self-sabotaging, second-guessing and not trusting her judgement. The feeling of low self-worth drains her whole being, leaving her wondering if she could feel any lower. The fear that holds her back – not being enough, people-pleasing – leaves her short with no time for fun or for self-care. These are clear obstacles and blocks she faces every day that stop her moving forward towards living a happier life because she feels there is no hope and does not love herself enough to make the change.

This can happen to anyone; even the singer Adele has made a huge career in writing and singing about failed and one-sided relationships. However, I understand that this can be very hard for you to believe when you have been truly wronged by the one person who you thought loved you, someone who used your love against you. By carrying on living your life with the same thought patterns and beliefs that do not serve you, your outlook on the world and your relationships with others – with your children and especially with yourself – will keep you on autopilot and repeatedly in survival mode.

'Michelle, I don't have the strength to make a change. I have no more energy to give,' I hear you say, and I want you to take this moment right now to just pause, put your hand on your chest… and breathe. At this moment, right now, I am sending you a huge hug of compassion, love and empathy. I see you – I truly see you– and I really do care that you find that release to let go of what is holding you back so that you can love life again. Together we can make your journey back to self-love, with ease, flow and with manageable mindfulness habits.

I have made mindfulness a daily practice in my own personal growth and family life for the last six years and have been coached with the best mindfulness coaches in the industry. Having suffered immense trauma from my emotionally abusive husband, and the public humiliation of him committing bigamy and it being broadcast around the world, I had lost hope in myself, my life and my purpose. I carried so much shame, anxiety and low self-worth that I did not want to carry on, and it was only when I looked down at my six-month-old daughter sleeping in her cot that I realised I did not love myself, so how was I even going to know how to love my own daughter? I wanted to escape the black hole in my mind, knowing that I had reached my lowest point, so the only way forward was to make a real change, while ensuring that I would always feel safe and calm along the journey. Developing a mindfulness practice provided me with a coping mechanism to manage overwhelming life challenges and a spiral of negative thoughts that created stories of judgement which clouded my mind in every decision I had to make for myself. I didn't trust myself, and feared the world around me.

Mindfulness has been scientifically proven to calm the nervous system down and relax the prefrontal cortex part of our brain, which can create the fog and 'monkey chatter' within our mind. When we focus on the present moment, we can create positive thoughts that motivate us to make changes to our negative thought patterns and to deal with difficult situations. Your mindset begins to develop an attitude of finding clarity in your thoughts and the root cause of why they are there. Being mindful opens your awareness to create a safe place to reflect on your choices, and not to act upon them impulsively, developing a sense of self-control.

I am here to tell you that there is hope, and it is truly possible to live a life with calm, happiness and joy. I am passionate about helping other women who have suffered with co-dependency, guiding them back to a point where they can love their life and feel like their authentic self – and we get to do it the fun, mindful way.

By creating small changes to your day, I will guide you to show up for yourself with fun, mood-boosting practices that find joy in the moment. I'm here right now cheering you on and telling you that everyone deserves to give themselves a second chance in life, including you! You are worthy of giving this opportunity to yourself, but only if you're willing to make a promise to commit, connect and work with a whole lot of self-compassion to make the shift within. The shadows of your self-talk are not true, and you are not your thoughts. However, those thoughts are there all the same, and you need to explore them with curiosity. You were not born into this world speaking unkind words towards yourself, so let's change this up. Talk to yourself with confidence, like the queen that you are.

This is my mission. I promise you that I will guide you back to your spark that has been hidden for so long. I am your biggest wellbeing cheerleader, rooting for you to gain the confidence you need to take your first steps towards getting your life back from co-dependency. We are about to start your journey back to self-love right now.

Chapter 2

My Story

In 2014 my world was turned upside down when I found out my husband had committed bigamy.

We got married in 2008, and like any newly wedded couple, we loved each other so very much that we were ready to start building a family together. Having a family of my own with the man I loved was all I ever wanted in my life, and the next step seemed natural: we decided to have a baby. My husband had been promoted at work to a new director's position within the company, which would mean he would need to travel and commit to working longer hours. Of course, I supported his decision, as this would help to build a comfortable life for us both.

However, this was when things started to change. He would be gone for more than two weeks at a time during a month; then he had to work nights, leaving me alone and missing him. He called me every day to check in, telling me he loved me very much, but I would feel frustrated that we hadn't spent time together, especially as we were also trying for a baby. Asking him when he would be home became a daily question – and he would say that he would be working late and that I needed to understand that he was doing this for us, allowing us to have all the things we wanted, so I should just lay off him for working so hard. When he was home, he seemed distant; when I asked him about his week, he would be vague and not engage with the conversation, as if I was not there.

Then one day in 2011 he called me to come straight home as he had something important to tell me. He sat me down and held my hands and told me that he had to go into witness protection. He said the company he was working for was connected to some sort of fraud investigation, so he and all his colleagues had to go into a safe house. I suddenly felt scared and confused, fearing for my husband's life and for myself. He comforted me by telling me he would be allowed to have a rare visit to see me, accompanied by a plain-clothes police officer. For my own protection, he told me I should not share this information with anyone, especially not our family or our friends – *no one* – as this would jeopardise everything. I now thought my life was in danger and started to feel suffocated in the isolation that I was now in. His visiting times with me had a two-hour time slot that was enough to have dinner and make love until he had to leave.

I was so sad, scared and lonely that I really couldn't believe this was happening. I kept asking him when it would end, and what the police were doing to end the investigation, but he kept telling me to be patient. I needed to understand it was not his fault; if I loved him then I should understand. I carried on going to work and living my life as normal, but my inner emotional state was all over the place. I wanted to tell someone about what was happening to me, and I was so stressed, filled with anxiety and holding on to so much pain. I made fewer dates with friends as I was always showing up on my own, having to make up excuses for him not wanting to attend so I didn't give anything away. He charmed my friends and, on the odd occasion he did show up, everyone loved him – he'd even pay for everyone's dinner. My girlfriends would say, 'Oh, Michelle, you're so lucky,' without having a clue what was really going on. I got very good at creating a mask that was very believable; having been an actress, I could put on a good act.

Then I had the best news – I was pregnant! If anything, that would get me thinking positively: we were having a baby. I told him about the good news over the phone, and suddenly, he went quiet. He said he was surprised, as it had taken us two years of trying. He told me it would be best that he was the one to tell his parents about the pregnancy, as it would be best to have as little contact as possible with them in the situation we were in. He continued to visit me when he could; when it was time to leave, there was always a driver waiting for him outside our home, who he told me was a police officer.

I needed him more than ever, but he could not be there. Six months into my pregnancy, I would lie in bed at night wanting my husband to hold me and tell me this nightmare would be over, and that we would be together soon as a family. He missed every experience in all the stages of my pregnancy – even taking part in the antenatal classes, where I continued to make excuses that my husband was absent, telling them he travelled a lot for work. It was just me and my baby.

In February 2014 my baby girl, Millie, was born. My husband missed most of the labour but managed to get to the hospital for the birth and to hold Millie for the first time. The nurse encouraged me to breastfeed my baby, but Millie was not taking to it, which upset me as I wanted her to naturally feed and connect with me. He told me to stop making a fuss and said I was being silly for getting upset, as I could just bottle-feed her. After his two-hour visit was up, he left, and I didn't know when I'd be able to see him again. Recovering from a c-section and exhausted from the labour and being left abandoned, I was feeling low with a newborn baby. The strain of receiving no support from my husband took a toll on my emotional state, leaving me stressed, frightened, and having to face this alone. I felt I was being punished for something, as this should have been one of the most memorable days of our lives. I thought we'd be going home together with a new baby, but I was on my own again.

It was the August bank holiday weekend, and I received an unexpected phone call from my friend. She told me she'd had a row with her boyfriend and needed me to come over straight away for support. When I arrived at her place, we left our kids playing and she took my hand, guiding me to another room. She held my hands tightly, looked me straight in the eyes, and told me she had something to tell me that was going to change my life: 'Michelle, your husband is living a double life.'

At that moment I think I stopped breathing, and a domino effect happened in my mind – the puzzle pieces all seemed to fit into place. I just looked at her, listening to the words coming out of her mouth but not really reacting at first. She then continued to tell me that my sister had discovered pictures of his other wedding day on Facebook. She wasn't sure at first if he was the best man or the groom, yet when she looked through the other photos – cutting the cake etc – it was clear he was the groom. As my sister lives a long way away, she couldn't come down and tell me, so she asked my friend who lived just up the road to do it.

I broke down in tears, feeling hugely betrayed and heartbroken. That's how he managed to do this! He lied and emotionally abused my trust, love, and all that I valued in a marriage. What a bastard! And while I was carrying his child, living my life and being a loyal wife, he had charmed and lied to everyone. It all made sense, but why had I not seen it? How stupid had I been? He was taking me for a fool and had made me feel like I was nothing.

I still have no idea how I got into the car with my six-month-old baby before driving safely back home. Not thinking straight and in a state of panic, I started to pack my bags. All I knew in that moment was that I needed to get away from there because I did not know who that man was any more. What I feared the most was the person who put fear into me. Why did this happen to me? I played it over and over in my head, and I cried for hours until no more tears would flow. My mind went into overdrive, playing over all the conversations, all the times he lied and the events he lied about so he could have his affair and his other life.

Somehow, I managed to gather my thoughts, but I needed to know how I would confront and deal with my husband, so I turned to one of my best friends, who had also experienced heartbreak and betrayal. She told me to get a good lawyer, who then advised me to turn him in to the police. From the day I walked into the police station, the arrest happened so quickly. They confirmed that he had committed a crime and were ready to arrest him at our home. I handed the police my house keys and they arrested my husband right there and then. That was the last time I saw or spoke to him.

I filed for a divorce straight away, but he did not make it easy for me. He delayed the process by not responding, which made it financially straining. Then, to add insult to injury, he served me with a demand for Millie to take a paternity test. That was the lowest of the low. How many more punches was he going to throw at me? In the 14 years of our relationship, I was a loyal partner, and my daughter and I did not deserve this. Of course, there was no doubt that he was the father.

When the trial date arrived, I felt I was living someone else's life, trying to get my head around what was happening to me, but I had the support of my loving family and friends who accompanied me to court. This was the first time I saw the other woman. The whole experience was a blur, and reading out my statement in court was the only chance I had to tell my side of events to all involved, explaining how this man had treated me. When the trial came to a head, he pleaded guilty.

From that day on, I was living in survival mode, trying to cope with the trauma caused by what my husband had done to me, the shame it had caused. In the UK, bigamy is very rare, so the significance of the case was huge. After the trial the media got hold of the story and hounded my friends, family and colleagues to comment on the events, which were becoming front-page news in every national newspaper. The attention from the media was so overwhelming for me. I was still trying to recover from my heartbreak and becoming a new mother while everyone knew about my private life and failed relationship. Somehow, I pulled myself together to give my side of the story, just so I could end this public humiliation.

I felt broken, ashamed and a lot of anger towards myself; the noise in my head built up so much anxiety that my self-esteem reached rock bottom. I didn't want to feel this intense pain that I was reliving every day. Was I not lovable? Was I not beautiful enough for him? What did I do wrong? How would I ever trust another man again? After everything I'd been through, I really questioned my self-worth. He had been controlling and emotionally abusing me, keeping me small, shutting me out from his family, so that he could carry on his hurtful secret for his selfish gain. I felt like a failure in all areas of my life, and I could not see any hope of regaining my happiness and finding love again.

So, yes, my lovely – it was as shit as it could get! However your heart gets broken by your toxic ex's behaviour, it damages that beautiful part of you. I am here to tell you how I got out of that mind-controlled state, found my light and began to shine again.

The next two years saw me running on autopilot, just getting through each day the best way I could by distracting myself and not dealing with the trauma. By keeping myself busy, smoking and giving attention to whoever would take it, I placed a Band-Aid on the wound I had inside.

Until one day, out of nowhere, while I sat at my desk at work, I felt an overpowering wave of emotion that hit me like a ton of bricks. My chest became tight, and my breathing was short and fast, like I was suffocating, and I started to cry… It was like I had no control over my body. I ran out of the office to get some air, still shaking – I was having a panic attack. I called my best friend to tell her what had just happened, and she said with compassion, 'Hun, you have been through so much. Do you feel you need help to heal?'

That was the point when I realised I needed to change; I needed to stop hurting myself and start my journey towards healing.

I heard that practising mindfulness and meditation was a good way to feel calm, and if anything, I really needed to slow down, both mentally and physically. I was lost in who I was, and what purpose I had in my life. I didn't know where to start or who to speak to, but I was willing to try to find a solution. I downloaded a meditation app on my phone and decided to plan in time to try it out that evening. If I am honest, at first, I had no idea whether I was doing it right. But I closed my eyes and focused on my breath, and it felt good. I made a promise to stick with it, and what I noticed was that it gave me a moment when I wasn't lost in my negative thoughts, focusing instead on connecting with myself and my body. Don't get me wrong – my bad thoughts did not just disappear, but the meditations guided me towards looking into why they were there without judging myself.

Six months in, and I was making meditation a daily practice in my life. Meditation allowed me to feel my emotions in a safe way, with self-compassion, while speaking to myself kindly. I started journaling morning and night, writing down what I was feeling and reflecting back with curiosity about what was the root cause of my pain, all of which began to give me clarity.

I started looking at my life with gratitude, and I was so grateful for all the love and support I had around me – especially my beautiful daughter, who was the sole driving force behind why I am still here today. I would still have good and bad days, but the difference was that I was not getting overwhelmed by them, letting them control me. Instead, I was focusing on being in the present. By taking a step back to pause and be calm, I managed the way I responded to what life threw at me. I woke up with the intention of just feeling good, and step by step, I was turning my life around. One day I just stopped smoking, just like that! I felt I didn't need it any more. I was planning more time for myself, doing what I loved on my own and with my friends, and I bought my first own home, which I had never thought was possible. I was smiling through my days more and having *fun*!

I started to explore a spiritual path and enrolled in classes that developed my personal growth, making a promise to myself that I would commit to my journey towards self-love. I was getting stronger, becoming more confident and loving who I was becoming, all by changing the way I looked at my life. With the wonderful benefits I was experiencing with mindfulness, I wanted to teach Millie how to become mindful, too, as I knew this would be a life skill she would benefit from as an adult. I typed into my computer 'How to teach children meditation' and, without hesitation, I enrolled onto a teaching course at Connected Kids. I had read case studies of children who suffered from anxiety and stress and were on the spectrum who found benefits from just feeling calm and relaxed. Teaching mindfulness to children was my new-found passion. I studied hard for two years while working a full-time job, and became a certified meditation and mindfulness professional tutor. I also wanted to bring movement into it, and qualified as a family yoga teacher.

When Covid hit in 2019, I was put on furlough. I decided to make my time in lockdown a positive one, by creating a family mindfulness platform on Instagram called Meditate and Shine. My intention was to start a business teaching families mindfulness and yoga to connect with each other in a fun, calm and relaxed way – and the best thing was that I got to do this with my daughter, who loved it just as much as I did. I created a five-week family programme called 'Shine Bright' that ran online on Sundays; much to my surprise, not only were the kids loving it, but the mamas loved the fun, relaxing sessions too. They would message me to say that the sessions made their children feel good for the rest of the day, and that they themselves felt better and were facing their day with ease. It was amazing to help these families connect with each other and develop a practice that would also manage the overwhelming emotions that were heightened during Covid.

Still committed to my ongoing journey towards self-love, the experience of lockdown and uncertainty over what the future held brought up some trauma that I thought I had dealt with, which gave me the sense that I was stuck and could not figure out how to heal on my own. So I reached out to my coach, who put me on a 12-week 'Burnout to Balance' coaching programme to dive deeper into my trauma. By the end of the course, I truly felt transformed, forgiving and fully accepting myself so I could finally let go of the past. I was ready to unapologetically go for my dreams and create a business that was meaningful and had purpose. I was so inspired by how transformation through mindfulness, positive thoughts and fun mood-boosting practices could truly bring me back to feeling like *me* again – but maybe even *better*! Life is fun, and I *love* who I am. I am stronger, I am enough, and I am worthy for all that I desire in my life.

I ran with this new-found love of life. One day when I was meditating, I felt this urge of purpose that I needed to help other women to heal through mindfulness, like I had. I knew my story could help others and show women who had been through tough times that they could heal as well. When I was doing the family work, I noticed the mums were the ones who desperately needed my help – they loved it.

I created my conscious coaching mindfulness practice under my own name. My clients are working mothers who have struggled with a lot of stress, anxiety and difficult relationships, giving to everyone else and needing to claim some time and space for themselves. Mindfulness helps them to do just that.

They mean the world to me, and seeing them transform to connect with themselves while gaining a new-found love for life truly is rewarding. One client left her husband, who was neglecting her needs, and found love again. Another found joy in her day through her love of cooking. Another client made mindfulness a part of their family practice as it brought calm to the frantic moments in their lives. But most importantly, *all* the women made time for themselves to do what they loved.

So, I was you! I have felt it and lived it! And I know exactly what is going on with you. My approach is to start where you are right now, and together we can create a mindfulness practice that is manageable, fun and unique to your lifestyle. We start with the relationship you have with *yourself* and look at the self-limiting beliefs that block you from moving on from the past. So, let's get started and find that light within you so you can SHINE bright!

Chapter 3

Myth Busters

Myth 1: Spending your time

'I don't have the time to do the work; I am a busy mother and career woman'

For sure, it feels like there's never enough time in the day to plan in time for you. However, you manage to plan in time to shop for food, plan in a holiday, text your family and friends back and keep yourself updated with life on Instagram and Facebook; it's a matter of what priority you give your self-care. There are ways to work around this when you become aware of how you spend your time. Can you honestly say you plan your time wisely? Or is it the case that you're just focused on getting through the day, ticking off your task lists? When was the last time you added time with *you* onto your job

"

It's a matter of what priority you give your self-care

"

list? Yes, I am guilty of this too, finding that life just takes over – but being self-aware, you can see where it's possible to plan in time for you in your day, week, or month. It may mean waking up half an hour earlier in the morning, planning in a mindful break within your working week or taking time for you when the kids are at the after-school club. Mindfulness is all about being present with yourself in every moment that you take time out for you; depending on what your needs are, really 10 minutes a day can be enough to work on you.

Myth 2: Doing the self-work

'Making a change in my life feels so uncomfortable, and feels too much like hard work'

I am not going to flower this up, hun – change can feel uncomfortable, become messy and be hard work, but it is more exhausting staying where you are, living in pain and fear and in survival mode. The secret is to not look at your self-development as work, but to find joy in your day with curiosity and not to judge your thoughts. When you give yourself time to pause, you will start to treat and talk to yourself kindly with a whole lot of self-compassion, accepting who you are. Healing can also feel like a breakthrough – joyful and very unapologetic when meeting your needs. Through mindfulness, you start to understand why you feel the way you do, and create healthier thought patterns that will encourage you to make better life choices. When beginning your journey, always work at a pace that is comfortable for you; there is no contest or race in healing. I am here to support and guide you to make your journey an empowering one, creating a resilience to change so you can live a life that is more peaceful. A mindful practice gives you a safe place to create a happier mindset and be the best version of you. Time helps heal everything when you commit to putting in work to develop inner growth.

Myth 3: Mastering mindfulness

'Mindfulness and meditation seems out of my comfort zone, and I'm not sure I can do it'

Being mindful is a skill you already have and do daily. What do I mean? You make choices in your life every day, choosing to make a decision that is right for you at that moment. Mindfulness is simply being present with yourself and exploring your thoughts. Anyone can do it; in fact, you may already be doing it without realising it in some parts of your life. Mindfulness methods are universal and they can be adapted to anyone's lifestyle, being done almost anywhere at any time. There is no right or wrong way to be mindful or to meditate; you need simply to breathe, not judge yourself and be present in the *now*.

Myth 4: Investing in your growth

'I financially can't afford to invest in my personal growth'

When it comes to investing in your self-care and personal

growth, there is no price too high; you should make yourself a priority first, so that you can love and support others and the ones you love. You would never question how much money you spend on food, as you know you need to eat to live. This should be the same when it comes to looking after the overall wellbeing of your mind, body and soul.

At the start of your journey, you can keep your investment small, as there are many free and affordable resources out on the web – from downloading an app to joining a community online, like my Shining Sisterhood. It is only when you are ready to make a commitment and invest in yourself that change will happen towards the goal you want to achieve for yourself.

So, in conclusion, making your self-care and personal growth a priority is the first step towards creating a happier life. When you start to put yourself first, you can begin to heal and let go of the past. You deserve to feel good, have fun and get excited in rediscovering yourself in your healing journey. You will look and feel more confident and develop a happy mindset that makes you smile again.

Chapter 4

Process

In this chapter I introduce you to my fun process that will take you from low and overwhelmed towards reconnecting with a happier you and getting excited about your future. You'll learn what it is, where it comes from, why it works and who it works for. I'll share how my clients use it to get themselves back on track and feeling good about themselves.

My programme has come out of my own experience of being in a toxic relationship, my healing journey and my training in mindfulness. It has taken me seven years to get to the level where I have learned to manage the stress and anxiety caused by the trauma I went through. Determined not to be beaten by my negative thoughts, and wanting to be a better mother for my daughter, I knew with the right guidance and support there was hope. By devoting myself to a self-love practice through mindfulness, I have developed a happier mindset, created a healthier lifestyle and made choices that have supported me to move forward in my life.

Committing to my self-growth and feeling the benefits of mindfulness, I wanted to integrate this into my family lifestyle and to help others. As I mentioned before, I enrolled myself in mindfulness and family yoga courses to teach kids mindfulness and meditation, where I developed an understanding of how mindfulness can create mental shifts and develop overall wellbeing. I enhanced my skills by creating bespoke guided meditations, integrating mindfulness with the use of sensory tools and spiritual mindful methods. These all led to me working with families and mothers over two years to get my teaching qualification in mindfulness. The results these mums and families got were astounding, and it was so fulfilling to see that the children and parents felt good about themselves, learning to become self-aware and how to feel calm. Gratitude became their new attitude, and their parents had happier children after each session.

Parents who reached out to me with children on the spectrum could not believe how relaxed, calm and focused their child became after one session. One mama told me it was wonderful to see that her autistic two-year-old son allowed me to give him a foot massage and stayed focused for more than two minutes. I felt such joy knowing I gave these children and families a moment to just feel good about themselves. Even my girlfriends started to approach

"It can be a very lonely,
fearful journey when
restarting your life
and rediscovering
who you are
"

me about which stress busters could help with their daily challenges, and how to plan in time for themselves in their impossible life schedules.

Women who were struggling to get their life back after a divorce or a past toxic relationship reached out for help about how to develop a happier mindset. They wanted to learn how to regain their confidence and trust in themselves and start over again, out on their own. Relating to how these women felt and the struggles they were facing gave me a purpose to want to help other women know that there is hope, and there is a safe way to face the pain they are holding and begin to love life again. Mindfulness is a life skill that everyone of all age groups can develop within their lives and feel the benefits towards their overall wellbeing. I am so passionate, and I care about helping other women who have experienced a toxic relationship, who are left coping with the trauma. It can be a very lonely, fearful journey when restarting your life and rediscovering who you are, so I have made it my mission to spread the joy of mindfulness, making it the main foundation of my coaching practice – along with a little sparkle of fun!

Now I am going to share the best part with you, on how mindfulness will add joy into your life. My coaching approach is one that creates a happy mindset, feels safe, is manageable within your busy lifestyle, and most of all is fun! I have designed five organic steps for the busy single mama and others to begin their journey from where they are right now and start to look at why they do not feel good.

You get to work at your own pace and rebuild your confidence, trusting in yourself and gaining the strength to move forward. My method does not feel like hard work. It is full of fun ways to rediscover what you love while connecting to the happier version of you. There are no big steps; instead it is about taking the right small actions to allow you to safely observe your negative thoughts and the unhealthy habits that are stopping you from creating the life you want. You deserve to be happy, my lovely! And I will be your fellow cheerleader, rooting for you all the way towards your fabulous future self!

So, let's get to it! Here are my five steps towards finding your sparkle and SHINE!

The five steps

★ **S** low down, babes

★ **H** appiness is a choice

★ **I** am doing me

★ **N** urturing support from my squad

★ **E** mbracing my fabulous future self!

Step 1: Slow down, babes

In this step, you start where you are right now and look at why you do not feel good. I will coach you to open up your self-awareness and observe your thoughts and emotions, teaching you mindful practices that will allow you to connect with yourself in a safe, calm and relaxed way. You will become more aware of your thought patterns by being present through guided meditations, finding clarity in them by journaling them down, and starting to identify the strengths and skills that make up the sparkling elements of who you are. You will learn to look at yourself with a lot of self-compassion, not judge yourself in the process, and rediscover what you want with curiosity. This is the first step that will allow you to get real with yourself, be honest and truly work towards the life you want.

Step 2: Happiness is a choice

We get to look at all the good things that are present in your life right now. I will teach you to develop a happy mindset through gratitude and identifying what makes you smile again. You get to be present with yourself and others around you, and live out your day focusing on what brings you joy. I will show you how starting your day with a happier mindset and the intention to create healthier habits to make you feel good can change your outlook and your life.

Step 3: I am doing me

In this step, you will look at self-care as fun, by making a date with yourself to do what you love. Using my self-love tracker, you get to plan time out for yourself, coming out of your comfort zone while learning to pause and gaining confidence. I will teach you how you can become resilient to change and how looking back on your younger self for inspiration can inspire new fun activities and a zest for life. You will start to feel the benefits of investing in your wellbeing, and you will start to thrive.

Step 4: Nurturing support from my squad

I will show you that you are not alone in your healing journey and that there is support and resources available to you. You will learn to reconnect in fun ways with your family and friends, and meet like-minded people by joining and creating a community. You will gain confidence and develop the trust to share your experiences, supporting yourself while feeling empowered by others who have also suffered with co-dependency.

Step 5: Embracing my fabulous future self

Now you are beginning to feel good and to embrace who you are, it is starting to feel like fun! In this step, you start to make your needs and wants a priority. Babes, you haven't even touched the sides in discovering what you can do and the fabulous life you can create for yourself. You will learn to continue to invest in your growth and believe that change is possible, regaining your confidence and identity while fully reclaiming your power from co-dependency.

Sophie's story

Sophie, 36, is a beautiful career woman who has everything going for her – a good job, great friends and a life any single woman would dream of – but inside she felt she was never enough. She was always in a place of busyness, so she never seemed to have time to just enjoy life and slow down. She was an overachiever, trying to be perfect in everything, and she defined her self-worth in terms of her work achievements and outside validation. Sophie would have days where she had planned so many activities into her schedule that she was always on the move, leaving no room to be fully present and enjoy the experience. In fact, it made her feel more stressed and anxious. Putting so much pressure on herself just made her feel unhappy; she found it hard to just pause and slow down and think with a clear mind.

When Sophie signed up to my SHINE programme, her intention was to gain more confidence in all areas of her work and personal life. Even though she was aware that she needed to trust and believe in herself more, she didn't know where to start. Open and ready to try to make a change in her life, she took a huge step back – slowing down and deciding to make happiness her choice by starting to make herself and her needs a priority.

She took part in my online support group, Shining Sisterhood, which nurtured her to offer her support and help her connect to her squad, friends and community. Sophie became open and vulnerable so she could share with the other women in the SHINE community, learning to incorporate a mindfulness practice into her daily life, with useful mindful tools, meditation and self-awareness exercises. She particularly liked doing the mindful walk exercise, which allowed her to use her senses and be present in the moment, as she also loved being out in nature. She learned how to manage her stress levels and take time out for herself to just truly have fun, which built up her confidence and meant she could start to love the woman she was becoming. In our one-to-one session, Sophie was able to transform her negative thoughts into thoughts of self-compassion through guided visualisation, meditation and journaling her feelings, with more kindness towards herself. Her energy became positive, and she judged herself less, starting to accept that she was not perfect and that was OK.

Fully embracing the SHINE experience, Sophie is now completely ready to embrace her fabulous future self and continue on her journey so that she can grow and shine more than ever before. Sophie is just one of the amazing women I have worked with; below are some others who share their experience.

Testimonials

Linda, 54

I found, through following Michelle's marvellous SHINE programme, a positive change in my routine to restore my sense of calm. It was easy to incorporate into my lifestyle, and Michelle's incredibly supportive and considerate approach has helped me to find better sleep, calmness and the return of my confidence. Thank you so much, Michelle!

Sarah, 36

Michelle is a calming, positive, encouraging, affirming coach. I was able to go through the programme at my own pace, which really allowed me to get the most out of it. I loved the SHINE programme, as it felt so nice to slow down and prioritise myself. There are lots of opportunities to self-reflect about who and where I am and what I want to be in the future. Thank you, Michelle.

Annabel, 34

Michelle is a fantastic mindfulness coach. She planned a one-to-one session for me where she led me through different mindfulness techniques. The session was invaluable at helping me through an incredibly difficult time personally. I couldn't have asked for more.

Carryl, 45

Michelle is so relatable, and the fact that this programme derives from personal experience means you instantly trust the process.

SHINE has left me feeling committed to continuing my new journey with myself because this isn't a quick fix, it's learning new habits to continue your journey towards an improved way of life. Whatever your age or stage in life, SHINE is perfect! Be curious and compassionate with yourself and go for it!

Chapter 5

Slow Down, Babes

My story: realising I had to slow down before I burned out

In June 2018 I had reached breaking point. I was stressed over getting my divorce finalised, working full-time, being a mother and facing difficult life challenges. I wanted to feel in complete control, tick every task on my list and be in a constant state of busyness, so that I felt I had it all together. I was being everything to everyone, not giving any time for me. Then one day, while out shopping with Millie, rushing to buy a last-minute birthday gift for a friend, I just stopped. I stood in the middle of the aisle and broke down in tears. I'd had enough – I was exhausted, my anxiety had reached sky high, and I just felt helpless.

Millie looked up at me and asked, 'Mummy, are you OK?'; I knelt, hugged her and replied 'No, darling, but I will be.' This was the point where I realised that things had to change. I needed to change, not just for my daughter, but for my own sake. I needed to give myself a break, learn to slow and calm down and feel less stressed. My trauma had caught up with me, and it was time for me to be brave and face it head on. But the first question I asked myself was: 'How?'

I felt so stuck I didn't know where to start. I could barely remember a time when I felt calm – it had been crazy for so long. All I knew was that I wanted to feel more at ease, to understand why I was feeling that way, and also to feel safe within myself. I was willing to try anything that would start to make me feel good and get me out of this survival mode before I completely burned out.

I heard meditation was a good way to slow down, calming the nervous system by using your breath. 'I can do that!' I said to myself, and planned to try it out that evening. I downloaded a meditation app and eased myself in with a five-minute guided meditation. I had no idea what I was doing or whether I was doing it right– but it didn't seem to matter, as I focused on just being present with myself through my breathing. I was not used to silence and at times my mind would wander, but the app guided me to connect with my breath, and not judge myself on the exercise, but to get curious about how I was feeling. I soon realised that there were areas of my body that felt uncomfortable, and just by breathing deeply, I could focus on those areas, allowing the tightness to become lighter and myself to become calmer.

Whenever I had moments in my day that overwhelmed me, I planned in 10 minutes to just pause, put my hand on my chest, close my eyes and focus on the rhythm of my breath to soothe me. This became my coping mechanism that I could do and use anywhere. I was beginning to look forward to taking time out for me so I could practise new breathing exercises, relaxing and feeling calmer. After three months of taking 10 minutes a day, I started to extend my meditation to 15 or 20 minutes as part of my morning routine. I would even focus on my breath on my drive when I was feeling a little anxious about the day ahead. I was feeling the benefits because my mindset started on a good note and I could take on my day in a calmer manner. This made me want to explore mindfulness practices more, learning how to manage my emotions and build confidence in myself.

Wanting to understand the way I was feeling and continue to feel good, the idea of writing my thoughts down through journaling gave me another tool so I could take time out for me to feel grateful for what was present in my life. I was grateful for family and friends, my home, my job, and the opportunity to start over and do the things I loved.

Six months after I became committed to the mindfulness routine, I started to look at my life as a happier one, with the possibility that I could create the life I wanted for myself and my daughter. Some days were hard – I would fall back into my old thought patterns of not being enough, and then self-doubt kicked in – but making time for myself to just pause, take a moment and breathe meant that I felt less pressure on myself. I was able to manage when I was being triggered in day-to-day challenges and not to be overwhelmed by them, as I was more self-aware of my feelings and beginning to identify what behaviour patterns I needed to change.

So, hun, what is the one thing you feel you need to change to start to move forward in your life? Maybe you know or maybe, like I did, you feel stuck in deciding where to begin. Don't worry– I've got you. So let's start our first step together, and that means starting where you're at right now...

What is 'slowing down' all about?

In this step, you will learn to slow down, take a step back and prioritise making sure that you have the time within your day to breathe and connect with yourself. We'll start to look at how you're feeling right now and observe why you do not feel good. The reason why this is the first step is that you have been living in survival mode, doing and being everything to everyone except yourself, and this will give you the opportunity to pause and take the time you need to calm down your stress and anxiety levels. When you start to slow down, you will be able to think and see things a whole lot more clearly. You'll also be able to identify your behaviour patterns (good and bad) that do not serve you, allowing you to make better life choices with confidence. You will understand how making your mental wellbeing a priority benefits not only you, but also the people who surround you. So today, let's let go of surviving and take the first steps towards thriving by slowing down, babes.

Why you need to slow down

★ **You're stuck in survival mode.**

Coming out of a co-dependent relationship can make you feel like you have failed. There might be feelings of guilt and shame about the relationship not working out how you imagined, but mostly you were dependent on them for everything– not just emotionally, but for security and financially. This creates huge stress to your mind and body when you start to venture out on your own, so you naturally go into survival mode. You're constantly in fear of what each day will bring and how you are going to make ends meet, and overthinking all areas of your life.

★ **You're easily overwhelmed because you're exhausted.**

Simple tasks like changing a plug, getting the kids' lunches ready for the next day, or prepping for that work project get too much to handle as you're thinking about tomorrow, and not focusing on what you can realistically achieve today. It begins to feel too much, and most days you just want to give up. However, in reality, you are exhausted and you have not given time to yourself to step back and pause, before mentally moving on to your next priority. In your mind, if everything is not done, you fear that you will lose control – which feels like it is not an option when you're a single working mother or career woman with children. I get it; it is tough, and it is hard, and you never know what life is going

By slowing down and allowing yourself to take the pressure off, you get to do more of what you want to achieve to throw at you at any given moment, but by slowing down and allowing yourself to take the pressure off, you get to do more of what you want to achieve.

★ **You may burn out the way you're going.**

When your mindset is clouded in overthinking, in self-doubt and fear, it makes it difficult to power through the small stuff, and you're easily triggered by the outside world. This is where 'being present' and taking time out for yourself will clear the fog in your mind so you can relax and think more clearly, understanding that how you are feeling is natural and that you will be OK. If you don't make yourself a priority, your thoughts and behaviour patterns will continue to spiral, which will eventually lead you to burn out.

Lucy's story

Lucy, 36, recently left her husband of six years, who had neglected her needs for him to be home more, spend time with her and support her in raising their two children. He thought she was being selfish, that she did not understand he was working hard for a life that was comfortable for them, and so he thought she should be more grateful. He was not prepared to change to make it work, as he did not see that there was anything wrong with their marriage. He believed she was lucky to have married a man like him.

Lucy constantly felt guilty about her feelings; she did live a life that she would never wish to leave, as her husband provided her with everything – except the emotional love and understanding that she so longed for. She had loved him very much and kept up the role of the perfect wife and mother until she confronted him, saying that she was unhappy and wanted a divorce. She moved out into rented accommodation not far from the family home so that her children could come and stay with her every other weekend. This added emotional stress and brought a huge change in her life, as she was experiencing loneliness being separated from them.

To be able to afford life on her own, she returned to her old job so that she could provide for herself.

This added financial strain to make ends meet and to cover court fees, as she was very unsure how she was going to make payments. She became scared that she could lose her children. Her family was upset with her decision, and so she felt very alone, with little support from her circle of friends, which now felt divided. Lucy felt helpless and angry at herself that she was in this situation; she feared she would be left with nothing, and she was scared of what her future would look like. She was emotionally exhausted, and her anxiety caused her to worry and overthink everything, as she was losing control of her ability even to think straight.

Lucy reached out to me after her friend had said I had gone through a similar situation. She had read in a magazine article that mindfulness and meditation was a great way to relax, release stress, and help to calm down anxiety. When Lucy came to me, she had reached a low point. She felt depressed, tearful and stressed, and wasn't coping with life on her own. Knowing what to do next to guide Lucy came easily to me, as I saw in her a reflection of what I had once been through. I looked at her with a lot of compassion and said, 'Today you are going to give yourself a break, hun, and know everything is going to be OK.' At that moment, I saw her smile for the first time.

I got her to focus on connecting with herself through a body scan meditation, which allowed her to become aware of any tension within her body. Using her breath and placing her hands on her chest and stomach, she focused on breathing into that space and softening the tension on the exhale to release it. The aim was to get Lucy to relax her whole body and mind and take a break from the stresses in her life. I asked her to focus on relaxing every muscle in her body, starting from the top of her head and going right down to her feet. This was a way for her to begin to connect to her body and feel any sensations in a safe way rather than being overwhelmed by them.

I guided Lucy through this meditation for 10 minutes until I asked her to open her eyes and give feedback on her experience. She was surprised how much calmer she felt, and noticed how focusing on her breath had allowed her to just relax. During the exercise, she had thoughts come and go, but found it achievable to reconnect and bring her focus back to the present. The overall result was that she felt good and calm!

From that moment on, I created a five-week bespoke mindfulness programme for Lucy with mindfulness practices that included journaling, meditations, mindful moments and self-awareness exercises which were manageable to plan within her busy day-to-day life. At the end of each week, we reconnected to reflect and explore what came up for her. She learned to slow down, and she recognised that she had not put her needs first for a long time but was now beginning to feel less guilty in making time to do what she loved. Lucy made it a priority to plan in time to journal every morning, as she found it beneficial to find clarity in her thoughts and find gratitude in each day, however overwhelming it would be.

Lucy got excited each week, eager to make time for herself so she could relax; she found that her energy levels were becoming higher, so that when her children visited she had the energy to be present with them and have fun. The exercises felt easy to her, and she could feel and see the benefits within herself as she was able to take a step back and face the day with less pressure and lowered expectations. Even her family and friends could see that she was starting to smile again.

During the court proceedings was when she felt triggered the most, as her husband was being unreasonable and making it difficult to finalise the divorce. Between court breaks, Lucy would find a quiet area to ground herself by closing her eyes and focusing on her breath to help her relax and manage all the emotions she was feeling. One year on from our first coaching session, Lucy is now divorced. She has found love in a new relationship and is planning to buy her very first home.

Witnessing my clients' growth and seeing them making it out on their own brings me so much joy that I have guided them back to their happier selves, to a place where they can start to create the life they want for themselves. You see! There is hope, and it is possible, but only when you allow yourself to put yourself first and slow down.

'So, where do I start to find the time to slow down, Michelle?' I hear you ask. The secret is to start where you are at right now, with small steps. This is not going to feel like hard work, because unlike the jobs on your task list, this one will feel good and guilt-free. You are going to give yourself the opportunity to make time to unplug and just relax. Can you remember the last time you took a break and just felt calm? … Are you still thinking?

Maybe you thought if you stopped doing, then you would lose control and begin to become fearful of what would happen if you didn't achieve and complete your day-to-day challenges. Because being in a state of busyness has become second nature and so familiar for you, taking time out to pause has never been an option. Let me be real with you: you will never get around to completing that list, as life will forever be adding onto it. When you start taking the pressure off yourself from survival mode, you will learn to feel more in control when you start to slow down. My darling, you deserve this time for you, as it has been a long time coming! If you never made time for your needs, this is the time to claim it now! Make yourself a priority. I will show you how, by connecting with your mind and body through your breath.

Exercise 1

Mindful me, myself and I

Step 1: Plan in your ME time

Plan in your calendar two days a week when you can take 10 minutes to give yourself a break; it could be one day during the week, and one day in the weekend. Decide whether you want time out first thing in the morning when you wake up, or in the evening when the kids are asleep. Time out can be planned for your lunch break, after a workout session, even when you're out taking the dog for a walk. There are no rules with regard to what time in your day you plan for yourself. This is the beauty of mindfulness: all you need to do is be present in the moment.

Step 2: Choose your space to relax

Choose a location or an area where you won't be disturbed with noise and can get comfortable. It might be an area in your bedroom, a guest room, your garden, or even somewhere that has the facilities to be a wellbeing room at work. It is important that the space creates an atmosphere that is quiet and has no room for interruption. For extra assurance that you won't be disturbed, you can hang a sign within your area or on the door to make others aware that you are having time out. I like to hang a dreamcatcher on my doorknob.

Step 3: Get comfortable

Now you have set the mood that will give you a time out, decide how you would like to get comfortable. You can sit on a chair, sit on a yoga mat cross-legged on the floor, or even lie down on the floor. Using pillows, blankets or an eye mask can give extra comfort if you need it. Again, there is no wrong or right way to position yourself, as long you have space that allows you to relax with ease.

Step 4: Pause, breathe and let go

Now that you are ready to connect with yourself for the next 10 minutes, I will guide you through a body scan meditation that will release your anxiety and stress levels and will lead to you feeling good. Allow yourself to pause, connect to the rhythm of your breath, and start to let go of the tension. 'Yes please, Michelle!' I hear you say… Let's get to it and enjoy!

Meditation: It's good to feel good

Hello, my lovely. Today we are going to give you the gift of taking time out for yourself. Take this opportunity to just relax and slow everything right down.

There is nothing to do right now, other than just be – be present.

Whatever you may be feeling right now, know that it is safe to feel it, and let it go. This time is for you to feel calm, relaxed and still.

This meditation requires you to lie down on the floor or, if you feel more comfortable, on your bed. Make sure you have enough room, lie back into the ground, and place one hand on your stomach and the other on your chest.

Focus on your breath and your hands going up and down in time with the rhythm of your breath. Feel your body sinking into the ground more and more with every breath you take. Start by focusing on relaxing your feet, with your heels feeling heavy on the floor. Relax your legs and thighs, and soften any tension you feel. Relax your abdominal muscles and chest and feel the soft rhythm of your breathing going up and down. Relax into this motion for a moment and enjoy the connection you are having with yourself.

Take two more breaths and shift your focus to your shoulders; soften your neck and allow your shoulders to feel open and free. Now focus on your face; relax your eyes, mouth, jaw and the space between your brow and forehead. Relax it all.

In this moment, allow yourself to embrace this relaxation and receive this gift of just feeling good.

It's good to feel good, calm and relaxed. If you find thoughts coming in and out, that's OK: note it, then release it.

I am going to give you space to enjoy this moment of relaxation and slowing down your thoughts for two minutes. I will mind the time and prompt you back.

Continue to take deep breaths in and out in this feel-good moment. Slowly coming back, feel proud that you have given this time to yourself, and remember that you deserve to feel good.

You are now going to come back to your body slowly by rubbing the palms of your hands together, wriggling your toes and slowly opening your eyes.

Now smile, babes, and continue to feel good for the rest of your day. X

To listen to my guided audio meditation, follow the link below or scan the QR code.

https://www.michelleagbulos.com/meditations

Top tip

Don't worry if your mind wanders or if you're doing it right or wrong – there is no right or wrong. It is normal to find it hard at first, remember it is just about being you and slowing everything down and softening your body. Releasing tension that you are holding in your body right now, means you can move to a better feeling that is more calming and relaxing.

Bonus exercise

Take a break outside or in nature with a walking meditation. Take a walk to your local park or woods and literally be one with nature, using your five senses. This exercise will make you focus on the now and allow you to be present in the moment.

Chapter 6

Happiness Is a Choice

My story: making happiness a mindset

In July 2018 my divorce was finally finalised on what was supposed to be a day of celebration. I felt nothing but fear and sadness. Why did I not feel happy or relieved that I was now free to move on with my life? I was officially out on my own, having to start again, uncertain what my future would be. I could feel the stress and the pressure I was putting on myself to have my life under control; it was making me feel so unhappy. How could I feel happy and positive now that I had the opportunity to start again and to create the life I truly deserved?

For 10 years I had made another person the priority. I was finding it difficult to identify my needs and to feel good. I had based who I was on this traumatic event, so I was making myself feel like a victim, which did not sit right with me. I couldn't see past being the woman who had been cheated on, whose face had been plastered all over the newspapers. I did not want my life to be defined by my past. How could I change this mindset of hopelessness to one that gave me hope to motivate me to keep moving forward? How could I be a good role model to my daughter? I wanted to change how I saw and thought about myself, becoming happy about who I was.

Journaling became one of my favourite habits. I did it first thing in the morning and last thing at night. I read that gratitude journaling was a lovely way to see your life at present with more appreciation, and I wanted to feel that there was hope so that I could be grateful for what I had in my life right now. I would list what I was grateful for in my day: things like my daughter, a roof over my head, not waking up with anxiety, the support of family and friends, the simple pleasures of getting away to my favourite woods, having a mindfulness practice and fun playtime with Millie. This attitude of appreciation instantly boosted my mood, and I started to look in reflection at how many things were good, and not so bad. Reading back my gratitude list made small shifts to my negative mindset so that it became one that was grateful, with less self-doubt and more hope, because what I was grateful for allowed me to create more of what I wanted. I got curious about how I could carry this happier mindset into my day.

Whenever I had a day that didn't go well, I would purposely step back, take a deep breath and run through my mind what I was grateful for on that day and what had gone right, rather than focusing on what went wrong. I was intentionally wanting to choose the next best thought, the one that would make me feel happier– and the best thing was, it didn't have to take much time. I could do this exercise anywhere, and it felt like fun! I was starting to look at my outside world with more hope, finding the small joys in my day, and I was smiling again. This new positive attitude felt organic to me, and I was beginning to get excited about the possibility of change.

Although I was making small shifts in my outlook on life, I still was curious as to why I was finding it difficult to feel happy being me. I was still feeling shame and anger towards myself, so I was learning to be more compassionate when I spoke inwards. There were days when I would look at myself in the mirror and use words that were unkind: 'It's your fault this happened; you were played like a fool, why did you not see it?' and 'Who would want you now that you are in your forties with a child? You're old and you're not beautiful enough'. Yes, that's how unkind I was to myself, and I knew it was not healthy. Exploring mindfulness, I wanted to change the way I spoke to myself so I could begin to gain confidence, strength and love in who I am.

Through my guided meditations, I used affirmations like 'I am strong', 'I am enough' and 'I am loved'. It felt very powerful, especially as I was not used to saying such words to myself. However, repeating the affirmations gave me a sense of belief that I was indeed strong, enough and loved. Whenever I caught myself saying unkind words to myself, I would exchange to positive affirmations to move on from my negative ones, which not only lifted my energy levels but also helped me to develop a happier mindset towards myself. I would write down these affirmations on Post-it notes on my mirror and repeat them back to myself so I could start my day on a good note. Even when I started comparing myself to the girls at work, I would speak inwardly to remind myself that I was beautiful and unique in my own way and, when I was faced with a difficult situation, I would use 'I am limitless in all areas of my life', just to regain my confidence. It was like I was faking it until I made it and believed it. My mental wellbeing was improving, and I was beginning to find my spark and shine! Would you like today to feel more upbeat, lift your mood and feel happier? Is the answer 'Hell, yes'? Let's start…

What is 'happiness is a choice' about?

In this step, you will learn that happiness is a choice you make by developing a happier mindset. At this point, you have made other people's needs more important than your own, and now it is time to give yourself what you need to feel good and smile again. This will be a practice in being present and seeing what is going well in your life right now. You will begin to look at your outside world with hope and appreciation, and start to look at yourself with a whole lot more self-worth.

Why you need to make happiness a choice

★ **To move on with positivity.**

Happiness is a choice, and it is no one's responsibility to make you happy, except yours. I know, my lovely, the hard truth is that you made your ex your everything, and that has left you disappointed and sad it didn't work out. I feel you, and I totally understand, as I have been where you are now. The thought of having a happier mindset feels like hard work, right? It hasn't come naturally for a while – but it doesn't need to be that way. You may have felt there was something wrong with you, that you were not enough for your partner, which was why they treated you so badly – but I am here to tell you that you are enough. You are worthy of being treated well and being happy. There have been so many distractions in your life up to now that you haven't given yourself time to see what is good in your life at present, because the fear of what the future brings either gives you more stress or heightens your anxiety, which leaves no room for happier thoughts. You still have it within you to make happier and healthier choices, even when your external world is not going the way you would like. Give yourself that permission for a moment to choose a happier mindset and claim back your power. By changing your mindset to one of gratitude and appreciation, the way you live your life will improve and you will be able to see the opportunities to create more of what you are grateful for, which leads to more happier thoughts.

★ **To stop putting other people's needs first.**

The main reason you are finding it hard to feel happy is that you have been making other people's needs a priority above your own. It may be that you haven't meant to make yourself your second priority (or even third if you have children), as it is in your nature to be kind and giving, but finding a balance in your mental and physical wellbeing is so important for you to be able to function as a healthy human being. When you start to fulfil your own needs, you allow yourself the time and space to pause to identify what you love to do that leads to a happier attitude. The attitude you have towards yourself will always be the most important, as you are the one who has to live your life as you.

★ **To start to look at yourself with self-love.**

That's right, hun: when you develop a happier mindset, you get to see yourself in a whole different light – one that sparkles! The self-doubts, judgements and comparisons with others leave you at a low point, not willing to shift the negative thoughts and the unkind words you tell yourself. I can tell you now that about 99.99% of us have been there, including me, but I also know that coming out of a toxic relationship heightens this mindset to a whole different level that is not healthy. You begin to believe that you don't deserve to have all that you truly want, because you feel shame and anger towards yourself. Your beliefs tell you that you are not strong or independent enough to make it out on your own, because you lack confidence and you hold fear that you will fail. Believe me when I tell you that you are not your thoughts, and that you are one hell of a badass woman who has been knocked back by a huge rejection from a person you thought loved you. You can claim back your power when you intentionally make small daily mental shifts in the way you think about and talk to yourself. You begin to look at yourself with the belief that you are beautiful, unique in your own way – and then you can accept who you are. This is so essential to creating a positive attitude that develops a happy mindset to start to move on from the past.

Bailey's story

Bailey, age 32, is a beautiful, successful career woman with whom I used to work in the fashion industry. She was in a relationship with her on-and-off toxic boyfriend, Toby, for two years. She tried many times to move on and cut him off from her life but found it hard to detach from him. There would be days when he would not call or message her back, and he even totally ghosted her for a month. But she found a way in her mind to make excuses for him, as she loved the way he made her feel. It only took him to say 'I miss you' and beg to give it another try for her to find herself running back to him.

Then one day, after a huge argument when she confronted Toby as to whether he was seeing another woman behind her back, he finally ended the relationship, leaving her feeling angry and depressed. She called work the next day to tell them she was unwell, when really, she didn't have the strength to get out of bed as she felt so low.

When Bailey met up with me for lunch a week later, her self-esteem was so low that it took her 10 minutes to get herself together from the tearful state she was in. I hugged her and told her she would be OK, that everything she was feeling was natural and there was nothing wrong with her. She continued to say that even though she knew Toby was toxic, she couldn't understand why she was finding it so hard to forget him; she needed to be back with him, which created a whirlwind of emotions that overwhelmed her.

I told Bailey that Toby was like an addiction she found hard to let go because the relationship was filling a hole: she was not loving herself and relied on his attention to validate her self-worth. I continued to tell her that there was hope and that by working together with me she would start to feel happy again. To get her back to a sense of ease, and to help her relieve the stress she was holding within her body, I asked her to close her eyes and pause for a moment to focus on her breath, just to slow down everything she was feeling. After five minutes focusing on a breathing exercise, she was feeling calmer and was able to think more clearly about what she could do next to start getting herself back on track.

Bailey told me she didn't want to feel sad any more, and that she didn't like herself very much, but she was willing to try to change. I told her, 'that's a good place to start.' For an hour, I talked her through a four-week practice plan that would fit into her busy schedule and lifestyle. I wanted the exercises to feel easy for her to do at any time and anywhere.

The first step was to get Bailey to see what was good in her life and to shift her mindset to a happier one, showing her that she is indeed a woman of value. Gratitude journaling was planned for her first week. Bailey was able to list 10 things she was grateful for in her day whenever she had a free 10-minute slot in between meetings or at night before she went to bed.

At first she found it easy to list what she was grateful for that she could see in front of her, but when she turned inwards, she started to feel grateful that Toby was no longer the first thing she thought of in the morning and the last thing at night. To make it easier for herself, she had a pen and notebook for the evening ready on her bedside table, and created a journal folder in her phone so that when she travelled to work by train she could jot down her list. She noticed the joy in her day through writing down her thoughts. She was taking steps to do more of what she was grateful for. She was grateful for her job which allowed her to pursue her passion in fashion and working on exciting projects. She was grateful for the time she gave for herself to work out in the gym, and she started to appreciate the weekend visits from her sister and playtime with her nephew, whom she loved dearly. She was grateful for her girlfriends, whom she had not seen for a while; now that she was not with Toby, she was spending more time with them, having fun.

We had weekly check-in sessions where I would follow up her gratitude practice with a guided gratitude meditation to connect with mind and body to lift her energy. By the third week, Bailey had moved on to guided affirmation meditations, where she repeated the affirmations back to herself with intention. At first this practice felt uncomfortable, as she had never spoken to herself this way, but by saying them over and over she came to love them so much that she stuck Post-it notes around her computer screen just to remind herself how amazing she was. Not all days were cheery, but the small shifts became big changes in the way she was seeing herself and feeling happier in who she was becoming.

It was becoming clear to Bailey, four weeks into her mindfulness plan, that she was blessed in her life and could see it and feel it for the first time. In the fourth week of her practice, she received a text from Toby asking how she was doing and if she would like to meet up for a drink to catch up. A message like this would usually trigger her to immediately respond and accept, but now she felt different and insulted that he thought she would go running back. She knew that the best thing was to ignore it and not reply, so she smiled and put her phone down. Bailey had worked hard and was beginning to love herself for the first time in a long time. She wanted to be in a relationship with someone who truly loved her. Through gratitude and positive affirmations, Bailey was able to choose again with a happier mindset that developed healthier habits, like learning to say 'no' to things that did not serve her. She took responsibility for her own happiness.

Wouldn't it feel good to start your day with ease and look forward to what your day will bring? Wouldn't you love to develop a mindset that brings joy to your day and makes decisions with positive intentions and motivations so that you can see all the good in your life right now? 'Yes, Michelle! I need this!' I hear you say... The next steps will feel like fun, and they will set your days off on a good note, moving forward to change your mindset towards creating more of what you want. Let's do this and start to make a shift in your attitude towards one of gratitude and positive self-talk.

Exercise 2

Gratitude is my attitude

Step 1: Noting it

Decide how and when you want to note down your gratitude moments – anywhere, at any time. You can have a journal by your bed or a journal folder on your phone or, if you are feeling creative, a pen and paper by a jar at home or at work to note down and put in your blessings. There is no set time or place to reflect on being grateful; just go with the flow and take time out to list them down.

Step 2: Moments of gratitude

List down 10 things in your life you are grateful for right now. It could be a person; a moment in your day that felt good or gave you joy; things that keep you safe, fit or healthy; truly, anything that makes your life easier and happier. There are no rules— this should be your very own unique list that levels up your mood or energy. The best things are the ones that just make you smile. A good way to focus and be in the moment is to close your eyes and breathe, reflecting on being present.

This exercise is to shift your focus onto a better, more positive thought, rather than dwelling on a negative one that holds you back, so that you can feel relaxed, calm and stress-free. When looking back at your list, identify why you are grateful and how it feels. This will connect to the feeling that makes you think happier thoughts.

Step 3: Create more of what you want

When you reflect back on your list of gratitude, pick one thing that you can make time in your week to do more of. For example, if you love to cook, why not extend that love by trying out a new recipe, or plan to cook dinner for family or friends. Not only will you enjoy it but the gratitude from others will come back to you and, ultimately, everyone will feel good all round; there is nothing more satisfying than feeling appreciated, happy that you made somebody else's day a little better, too.

Top tip

You can break down your gratitude list into sections (home, friends, hobbies etc.).

Exercise 3

Self-love affirmations

Step 1: Choose how you want to see your reflection

This exercise requires you to look at your reflection in the mirror – either a handheld mirror or your bathroom mirror, whatever is available and comfortable for you.

Step 2: Focus on how you want to feel

Close your eyes, place one hand on your chest, and imagine a feeling or emotion that would automatically make you feel better in this moment. It could be to feel you have more strength to get through your day, to feel beautiful in your body, to feel worthy enough to go for that new job you're applying for. Whatever the feeling, visualise it and imagine how you would look and feel.

Step 3: Begin with the intention of 'I am'

Open your eyes, look straight into the mirror, and say out loud each of the following 'I am' affirmations five times, slowly and with intention. Don't rush. Believe that what you say is true.

★ I am strong.

★ I am beautiful.

★ I am enough.

★ I am worthy.

★ I am loved.

★ I am safe.

★ I am limitless.

You may feel uncomfortable looking at your reflection while speaking these words out loud; you may even get emotional. This is completely normal, and it is safe to let go and release the self-limiting beliefs you have been holding on to.

Step 4: Fake it to believe it!

Yes, that's right, babe – fake it until you believe it, because it is the truth. The way you speak to yourself is powerful, and affirmations are a way to take the first steps towards a happier and more loving mindset.

Top tip

Be your very own cheerleader. I put my
affirmations on Post-it notes and stick them
around focal areas at home or at work. I like
to see those positive sparkles on my mirror
first thing in the morning or stuck around my
computer at work.

Meditation: Loving kindness meditation

Get comfortable in your meditation space, sitting on the
floor or on a chair, and focus on getting grounded and
connected with your body. Now take one deep breath in and
out and release the tension in all the parts of your body –
from the top of your head all the way down through the
chest, tummy, womb, legs and all the way to your toes.

This is the time to get connected with yourself and get
curious. Don't judge yourself. Take a few rounds of breaths
to focus, before letting go and just relaxing. Embrace each
breath with loving intentions. If you find yourself drifting
to other thoughts, just note them and let them go. Get
connected to the rise and fall of your breath, and get curious
about where it takes you.

Now think of a person – a friend or a member of your family, or maybe someone you know who is less fortunate than you. Visualise that person now.

Who is the first person that comes to mind? How would you want things to be better for them? What does it feel like? Would it be simply a way to support them, help them or be open to just listening to them? How would you show kindness and compassion towards them? How would you make them feel that they mattered? How would you make them feel that they were not alone? Breathe into that feeling; where do you feel it in your body? Take a moment to just feel it.

Now repeat silently to yourself: 'May they be happy, may they be safe, may they be healthy, may they be loved.'

Now reflect the same kindness back upon yourself. How would you show the same kindness to yourself? You matter, you are loved, and you have so much love to share. You deserve happiness. Happiness is your birthright.

I will mind the time, and I want you to just sit for two minutes with that feeling and embrace it.

Take note of how it feels, and just embrace it. Know that you are safe to feel it. Just breathe into each loving breath with the affirmation, 'I am happiness, and happiness is my birthright.'

Breathe in and out and note silently to yourself, 'I give myself the compassion I need. May I learn to accept myself as I am. May I forgive myself, may I be strong, may I be patient, may I be loved.'

Now, coming back to your body, wriggle your fingers and toes and rub your hands together. Take one more deep breath in and out, and smile.

To listen to my guided audio meditation, go to the link or scan the QR code below.

www.michelleagbulos.com/meditations

Bonus treat

Motivational podcasts are a fun way to inspire your personal growth journey. My favourite and suggested podcasts include:

★ *On Purpose* – Jay Shetty

★ *Feel Better, Live More* – Dr Rangan Chatterjee

★ *The Diary of a CEO* – Steven Bartlett

★ *Dear Gabby* – Gabby Bernstein

Chapter 7

I Am Doing Me

My story: rediscovering the fun in me

By 2019 I was embracing my self-love journey through committing to a mindfulness practice that allowed me the space to make time out for myself to heal from my past. However, I found it difficult to detach from my old ways and the patterns of my past life with my ex. For so long, we'd been making decisions as a couple, creating what our future would look like, and what I would need to change or work towards so that I could achieve that goal. But now I was trying to plan a life on my own, which felt unfamiliar and blurry. I asked myself, 'Who am I on my own?'

This thought stopped me in my tracks, because in that moment I didn't know the answer. I felt lost and upset that I did not have a purpose in my life. This did not make me feel good, secure or confident; in fact, it added more fear. It was like I had based my whole identity on being in that relationship, to the point where I didn't know who I was any more. 'Who am I? What do I like? What am I good at? When was the last time I did anything I loved on my own?' All this made me feel stuck, until one day while I was watching a music video with Millie, we just jumped up and danced.

We were both bouncing up and down, holding hands, shaking our bodies and laughing at how we were both out of rhythm with each other. When the song ended, we hugged each other, and went on to the next song to dance again. In that moment, I remembered how dancing made me feel and the joy of just expressing myself through movement.

In my younger days I was very shy, but somehow dancing gave me the freedom to express myself and have fun with it. In fact, my first career was performing in the musical Miss Saigon in the West End; reminiscing back to that moment gave me the idea that I wanted to feel that way again, having that sense of fun, being confident and free. I immediately looked up dance classes in my area and booked for a Wednesday night contemporary class.

'What are you doing here? You're not 21, Michelle,' I said to myself as I walked into the dance studio, seeing girls half my age warming up. But something within told me to stick this one out. The class began, and I just took a deep breath and had a word with myself: 'Michelle, just have fun.' And I did just that. The teacher got us moving all in sequence on the floor and all around the studio, and the sound of the music boosted my energy levels and released my happy endorphins. It was so much fun, raising my confidence and allowing me out of my comfort zone; I felt like I was 21 again. Even though I was not so quick in picking up the routine, I felt so proud that I showed up for myself and took the time out for me to move my body and to do something I loved.

However, it didn't stop there... As this feeling of taking time out for me fulfilled me, I got curious about what else I could explore that would nourish my mind, body and soul. I developed a new-found love for spirituality and experience-conscious yoga (like kundalini yoga) and listening to motivational podcasts on my way to and from work. I was feeling and seeing the benefits that all this fun-time activity was offering, building my confidence and making me feel good about myself; I was now finally looking after me and my needs.

As I was embracing my own healing journey, I developed a passion to get involved in mental health awareness in schools. I applied for the 'Now and Beyond' mental health festival event, where I got to teach mindfulness at a school in my area, and continued to raise awareness for a mental health foundation charity by jumping out of a plane! Bonkers, I know, but I would never have known or believed

I could do such wonderful things if I didn't just go for it and show up for myself. I was loving the woman I was becoming. I had found a new purpose in my life that was meaningful, helping others – and it was so much fun, too!

The lesson here is that I chose to make time for something I enjoyed that didn't involve anyone else but me. That built up my confidence, took me out of my comfort zone and allowed me to take the steps I needed to start rediscovering me.

What is 'I am doing me' about?

In this step, you get to show up for yourself by taking self-care to a level that is fun! You get to make those happy endorphins flow by planning in time to do what you love. You get to do you in a way that is guilt-free, by creating hobbies and new skills that boost your energy levels and release the stresses of your day. By increasing your wellbeing through fun activities that relax your mind, body and soul, you rediscover your strengths and develop the skills that build up your confidence, taking the right steps to come out of your comfort zone by making time in your week just for you. This section is where the fun begins, and you get to date yourself in your best and most important relationship – the one with yourself!

Now that you are the
boss of your own world,
you get to plan in that
time to date yourself and
have fun

Why you need to plan in time to do you!

★ **To release your old identity from the last relationship.**

When you have been co-dependent with another, all your needs have been based around creating the foundation of the relationship, which now no longer exists, and parts of you (if not all of you) feel like they are missing that. This is normal. But depending on how long you were in that relationship, you have now realised how you never spent time on your own to do what you love, or were never given the space to. Now that you are the boss of your own world, you get to plan in that time to date yourself and have fun.

★ **To build confidence in yourself again.**

You might have depended on your ex for validation in the way you looked and felt, and how you lived your life. By taking small steps that feel fun, you begin to gain confidence within yourself. Plus, by trying out new things, meeting new people and discovering your strengths and skills, you will achieve things you never thought you would be able to do (like me jumping out of a plane). When you start trusting yourself again, you become more resilient to the change of making it out on your own, and so you take the necessary steps to make the investment in your overall wellbeing, which makes you feel great!

★   **To make time for what you enjoy.**

When you plan in the time to date yourself, it lifts your mood and releases the stresses of the day, meaning you will reap the benefits and want more of it. When you feel the benefits of having fun, not only will it make you happier, but your children and the people around you are going to feel that happiness too. Remember: 'a happy mama has a happy child'. Believe it or not, children are very much in tune with people's energy and, more often than not, match it. To make this doable, plan your childcare a week in advance and ask for support, as planning in this time for you will give you something to look forward to. Taking the time out will become a treat and a gift that you give to yourself– and who doesn't like a treat that is not only fun but beneficial for your whole mental and physical wellbeing? Repeat after me: 'Girls just wanna have fun!'

Christine's story

Christine, a 45-year-old full-time mother to four boys and part-time actress, is a devoted mother and wife. On the outside, she looked as if she had it all together, but she was constantly feeling exhausted, which left no time or energy for herself. Her hectic schedule involved making sure that everyone in her family got what they needed, getting the boys to school and the youngest to nursery on time, while auditioning for TV work and making sure the family home was in order. She loved her family dearly, but the overwhelming challenges of life, and constantly giving and making everyone else a priority, left no room for Christine to take care of herself and her needs.

She felt like she was running on autopilot, and the only time she got to pause was watching her washing machine spin for almost an hour. She couldn't remember the last time she made time to do what she loved, took time out to relax, spent time with her girlfriends or simply treated herself to getting her nails done. All of that seemed like a luxury and, having financial struggles, she felt guilty over giving that to herself. Having had failed relationships in the past, she learned very quickly how to survive; she had raised her first child on her own. Now with her present husband – a loving and supportive man – Christine still found it hard to feel enough for everyone, including herself.

When Christine came to me, she desperately wanted to feel like the woman she used to be before she became a mother: a woman who was full of spirit, who loved to dance and had time to learn new things. In a household filled with masculine energy, she wanted to feel feminine again, and not to feel numb with stress, anxiety and negativity. It was obvious that Christine had not made her own wellbeing a priority for a long time, and that she didn't know where to start. When she came to me, I asked her what her main intention was in wanting help, and she answered, 'I want to create space for myself to do more of what I love, and make my self-care a priority so that I can be a happy mama and wife.'

Being mindful of Christine's schedule, I didn't want to add any more tasks for her to feel pressurised into doing, but I wanted to pivot her mindset and have her plan her own self-care into the family schedule in line with everyone else's needs. I told Christine, 'It's time you planned in a date – a date with yourself.' You can imagine her expression when I told her this; she looked at me as if it was an impossible task. I just said, 'Babe, it is time that you started doing you!'

I gave Christine a balance exercise to plan in dates every other week that would fulfil her mind, body and confidence. The aim of the exercise was to reflect on what she loved to do, which then turned into identifying her needs, showing her what would fulfil her and make her feel good. She embraced the task and, with full commitment, wrote a list of fun things that focused and nourished her mind, body and confidence. Each activity could be something she did for as little as 10–15 minutes, or something she planned in for a day or a whole evening. Whatever she decided, she took ownership in making space and time for herself and made her family aware when she would plan it in. Christine used my self-love tracker to plan in her dates weekly and felt excited knowing when she would be creating space for herself.

Christine booked herself in for a dance class, took time out for her mental wellbeing with my guided meditations, and built the confidence to start a new skill by learning to play the piano. The benefits she got from this included that she was beginning to feel sexy in moving her body through dance, feeling a lot less stress, sleeping better and working towards her grade 1 exam in piano. With all these exciting new activities she was introducing into her life, for the first time she felt that she mattered. During our one-to-one sessions, she would share how making herself a priority boosted her mood, confidence and self-esteem.

To keep up the momentum, I would guide her through a visualisation meditation on how her life would be different if she continued to give time for herself, and what that would look like for her. Even her husband and sons were noticing how Mummy's new high-vibe energy made her happy and, with that, they felt good around her too. She was glowing and feeling less overwhelmed in her life and wanting to discover what more she could do to grow. She found by relaxing more that job opportunities arose, and she felt at ease in applying for them. She bought books on dance recovery to widen her knowledge on dance, and books on manifesting a life you want to create.

Due to her family lifestyle, there were times when she had to travel, but she just adjusted her plans to make it work. For example, she had to travel to a location where her son was filming for a TV programme, and planned in her meditation time in between her son's takes, which worked well as a way of remedying the stress of being on standby. Christine started to treat herself like the person she wanted to be, and it was working, and she felt like she was living on a natural high. Three months on, Christine passed her grade 1 piano exam and continued to learn outside of her comfort zone and make time for fun.

So, my starlight, if Christine – a mother of four boys – can plan in the time necessary to make self-care a priority, so can you! Let's go and have fun and make a date with you!

When you make your self-care a priority, you start to become more resilient to the changes that you are facing alone in creating the life you want. It is so important to keep on top of your mental and physical health, so that you are able to keep yourself strong and look after your family. You will start to glow differently and will look forward to just spending time on your own. Fun comes in different forms – chilled out, creative, physical or trying something new. The key is to regain your confidence, discover your full potential and rediscover the better version of you – the one who is happy and fun!

Exercise 4

A date with me

Step 1: Write down your ultimate fun time list

Grab a paper and pen. Draw three columns and title them Mind / Body / Confidence. Under each heading, write down a fun time activity that you can realistically plan in the day or the evening within your week. Be unapologetic about your fun time guilty pleasures – and the activity can be as big or small as you like, from taking time out with a cup of tea and a good puzzle to skydiving out of a plane! Remember that the aim is to plan in time for you, build up your confidence, boost your energy levels and start coming out of your comfort zone.

Download worksheet: **www.michelleagbulos.com/exercise1**

Step 2: Plan in your date night with YOU!

Plan in your week one of the fun time activities you can do during the day or in the evening. For consistency, I would suggest that you should block out the same day/time each week, so that you are committed to your self-care. If life gets in the way and plans need to change, don't be hard on yourself; just re-plan for another day or the next week. Remember, you need this time for you.

Step 3: Do it, feel it, write it

To wind down from your date with you, this step gets you to note down in your journal how you felt during your activity, and why it felt good. What were the benefits? How did you feel? And why would you do it again? You may have found that you learned something new, or that it was physically challenging so you wanted to do more of it, or that it simply felt relaxing. There are no right or wrong answers, just small steps taken towards understanding what your needs are to feel good again.

Top tip

Consistency is the key to feeling and seeing the benefits of taking time out and trying out new things. Making the time for your self-care will become second nature, because at this point this is the first step in fulfilling your needs and your overall wellbeing.

Meditation: Shine, baby, shine!

Today, my lovely, we will connect with your shining energy within that makes you the unique queen that you are. You are amazing, you are loved and you matter, and when you fulfil your needs, then you become confident, strong and fearless.

Get comfortable and relax, and start to soften your body, starting from the top of your head right down to your toes. Imagine a warm golden light passing through your body, lighting you up like a star. The more you breathe in and out, imagine the light getting brighter and brighter. This light symbolises all the greatness you hold and share with the world.

The light feels warm and safe, and covers your whole body like a blanket. Embrace this relaxation and the comfort it gives you. Within your light, you are not afraid to shine. It gives you strength, confidence and acceptance of where you are now and who you want to become.

In this light you unapologetically visualise all that you want and who you want to become. You are unstoppable and limitless in all areas of your life. Embrace where it feels in your body, feel this energy – find focus and take a deep breath in and out and release it out into the world – and again.

Now repeat quietly to yourself the mantra, 'I matter, and I am not afraid to shine.' Do this for two minutes.

Coming back to your body, wriggle your toes and fingertips.

To listen to my guided audio meditation go to the link or scan the QR code below.

www.michelleagbulos.com/meditations

Bonus treat

Treat yourself to my favourite personal growth books that have influenced my healing journey:

★ *Find Your Mama Groove* – Joanna Hunt (for mamas)

★ *The Universe Has Your Back* – Gabriella Bernstein

★ *A Radical Awakening* – Dr Shefali

★ *Doing The Work* – Nicole Lepera

★ *Inwards* – Yung Pueblo

Chapter 8

Nurturing Support From My Squad

My story: building and reconnecting with my squad

My friend Layla invited me to her daughter's birthday party, and I was having second thoughts about attending as it was going to be a big gathering. The thought of facing others and starting up conversations scared me, as in my mind everyone already knew my story as the woman whose husband committed bigamy. I didn't want to get stuck in an awkward moment.

I arrived at her home and, as I expected, the party was in full swing, everyone chatting and enjoying themselves. I could feel the anxiety building up inside of me, and I avoided eye contact at all costs. I grabbed myself a drink and took Millie straight to the bouncy castle in the garden. I started to judge myself, saying, 'I am the only single mother here, and everyone is looking at me.' Of course, that was not true, but it felt like it. Layla came over and gave me the biggest hug and said she was so happy to see me, as it had been a while since we had seen each other. It was true. I had been so involved in my own life that I had isolated myself from her and my other girlfriends. She insisted that we catch up soon, and would not take no for an answer, so we planned to meet up for coffee in the coming week.

When I met up with Layla, she made sure we would not be disturbed and had my favourite coffee ready for me. She smiled at me and then said, 'Now, I want you to talk to me.' I started to apologise to her that I had not been in contact for a while as I needed time for myself to heal. I told her that I felt so alone and that no one would really understand what I was going through and I didn't want to sound like a broken record. When I stopped talking, she grabbed my hand and said, 'But I do understand, and you are never alone.' At that moment, I realised that she did understand, as she too had been hurt by a toxic ex-partner and knew exactly what I needed – someone who would just listen and reassure me that I was not the only one who had been through this, someone who had felt the same way. We talked for hours, catching up on each other's lives, and Layla told me the best news: that she was pregnant again.

I went home that day feeling so grateful for having Layla in my life and a little guilty that I had not checked in with her more often. I loved that she just listened, and I loved the way I felt at ease to share the vulnerable parts of me without judgement – it made me feel safe. That's what I loved about Layla – she had the ability to listen and give great advice, a quality that I had always valued in her as a friend. That evening I got curious about how my other friends were doing and planned in some time that evening to contact each one of them.

I called my mate Dan, as he was my go-to friend for fun and dancing. I texted my friend Alex, who had the same interest in theatre, shopping and trying out new restaurants. I removed the mute button from my mamas' WhatsApp group, who all love a good catch-up and having outdoor adventures with the kids, which fulfilled my need to connect with my mama role. In fact, planning in time with my friends was providing the support that I needed for my social wellbeing. I was grateful that most of my friends were very understanding and were happy to start where we'd left off. Some of my friends found it hard to offer support, as my situation triggered them – they also had areas within their mental health that they were working on. I found that sad, but I also understood that some people find it hard to deal with huge emotions, and difficult situations can also be overwhelming for them – and that's OK. I was learning and recognising each of my friendship groups' strong qualities, seeing that we were able to support each other, reconnecting and developing stronger relationships.

While reconnecting with my friends provided me with balance in my social life, I knew they were not qualified to help or support me in the deeper part of my mental health that needed healing. I was still struggling to balance life and motherhood. I was feeling burnt out all the time, and I wanted to know if there were other single mamas going through the same thing. I reached out to an empowerment mama coach, Joanna, after reading her book on burnout to balance and on finding your groove. Her methodology resonated with me, and I decided to take the step to join her programme. I had never had a coach before and knew there would be a huge investment in signing up with her, but I felt ready to do it for me. Her one-to-one sessions allowed me to face my fears and look deeper at the root cause of my limiting beliefs, and how I could face each day with more calm and balance. I worked with her for 12 weeks and connected with other mothers on group sessions who also suffered with burnout. I cannot begin to say how empowering and inspiring it was to connect with other women going through the same thing. Being in this community where we could be vulnerable and open to sharing our fears in a safe space was a game-changer, because I did not feel alone, and I wanted to support them as well as they were supporting me. I felt understood and not judged, which gave me huge comfort.

I now had a squad that was nurturing and supported my overall mental wellbeing, in the form of my friends, my coach and other women going through the same experience. I was building new and healthier relationships and getting

"

Leaving a co-dependent relationship and starting again out on your own can feel very lonely

"

the right support to fulfil my needs, developing connections with others while not feeling like a victim. I was a woman who was making my overall wellbeing and my relationship with myself a priority.

What is 'nurturing support from my squad' about?

In this step, you will learn to identify what type of support you need, what resources are available to you, and who to reach out to within your squad. I will provide you with exercises to help you create a squad that is fun, supportive of each other and empowering. You will benefit from being part of a community while building healthier relationships.

Why you need nurturing support from your squad

★   To understand that you are not alone.

Leaving a co-dependent relationship and starting again out on your own can feel very lonely, especially if none of your family or friends has ever experienced it. You feel that you are the only one going through this, and that no one understands. It is totally normal to have these feelings of being overwhelmed and lonely, but my darling, you are not alone. There are so many women who have experienced a toxic relationship at some level and have felt ashamed to seek out the support they needed, in fear of feeling judged and misunderstood. A problem shared is a problem halved, and when you start to support yourself and create a squad that offers comfort, safety and compassion, that's when you can start to heal and find the strength to move on.

★ **To reconnect and find support for your needs.**

You may have isolated yourself from others and lost connection within your circle of family and friends, so maybe you feel unsure how to reconnect again. Reaching out and not knowing how to approach a friend might feel awkward, and you may fear that they could reject you or have simply moved on. I have found that most people are forgiving and, when both parties are understanding about why space was needed, together you can decide how and when you are both ready to continue to rebuild the relationship. When a reconnection is made, you may both be surprised how rekindling a friendship makes it stronger and better than it was before.

★ **To be part of a sisterhood that empowers and inspires your personal growth.**

As humans we need to feel connected in all areas of our life, and as women when we socialise, grow together and share each other's healing journey, we feel empathy when sharing personal experiences. When you join a community that allows a safe place to connect without judgement, it empowers confidence and nurtures your personal growth. The energy you feel when women support each other gives a sense of belonging and a strong understanding of acceptance within the community. Being part of a sisterhood community that makes you shine creates a feeling of fellowship and connection in an inspiring squad. Without a squad you will feel forever trapped in a bubble of loneliness while never understanding your feelings.

Here are two of my shining babes, Linda and Sylvia, and their stories about how they connected and reconnected with their squad.

Sylvia's story

Being beautiful, single, and a career woman in the world of fashion all played their part in allowing Sylvia, 35, to look and act independent and confident. However, her internal world couldn't have been more different.

Suffering from self-doubt and a lack of confidence, while never feeling worthy of aiming for more, most of the time Sylvia sabotaged herself whenever she feared something would not work out. Her schedule was intense and really did not leave time to focus on her wellbeing, as she was constantly on the go. This came from being an overachiever and being a perfectionist; she didn't like not being in control of her life. When Sylvia enrolled in my SHINE programme, she hoped it would get her to slow down and gain confidence and trust in herself. It was essential that the programme would fit into her busy lifestyle, so that she would not feel overwhelmed and pressurised into completing it, trying to avoid feeling like a failure. I advised her that she should only work at her own pace and that healing was not a race, but a journey towards self-love and acceptance.

Being quite introverted and a busy career woman, Sylvia never had time to connect and build real friendships. In fact, she was never 100% happy connecting or letting people into her life so they could know the real Sylvia, fearing that they would not like what they saw. So, when week four arrived (the online 'nurturing support from my squad' group session), Sylvia wasn't quite sure she would feel comfortable sharing her thoughts and feelings with other women she barely knew. She messaged me to say she might not join as it seemed a little overwhelming and way out of her comfort zone. I said that it would be a shame, as connecting with other women who were going through the same healing journey would be so beneficial and empowering. Hoping she would change her mind, I said I would still send over the link in case she decided to join in.

The day arrived for my clients to meet for the first time online, and I was very excited to hear about how the journey through my SHINE programme had been for all of them. One by one they joined in; there was no sign of Sylvia, although I still had hope she would appear. Christine shared how the programme inspired her to want to change and create a better life for herself and her children. Linda shared how the resources offered in the programme allowed her to plan in space and time to feel calmed when she was overwhelmed. Lucy shared how scared and vulnerable moving on after her divorce had left her feeling. She spoke of how following the steps in SHINE gave her manageable ways to slow down and start to move forward by putting her own needs first.

One by one, each woman shared her stories and experiences, each moving, inspiring and lifting the others up, with encouragement and no judgement; they were just supporting and cheering each other on so they could all keep progressing along their healing journey. When I thought everyone had spoken, I could see Sylvia's window on the screen. She had been online all this time. I asked if she would feel comfortable in sharing her experience of the programme with the group.

A little hesitantly, she started sharing how it was her intention to gain confidence in all areas of her life. She thought that she was not good at anything and felt a little guilty that other women on the call who had children and other people in their lives managed to keep in line with the programme weekly, as she had barely made it to week three. She shared that she would plan in sporty activities and new hobbies in her schedule when she was not working and, due to the timing of classes, it made it hard to actually stop, pause or slow down. She continued to share that the reason she kept herself busy this way was that she felt average as a person and wanted to feel interesting and skilful. Inside, she felt like people were judging her as she was always judging herself.

When she finished, I could see that the rest of the group felt empathy for Sylvia and thought that she was being very hard on herself. Linda and Christine spoke up first to give words of comfort to her, saying that it was incredible and inspiring that she was learning and doing all these activities, as they certainly didn't know how to do bouldering or half of the activities she was learning. Other members continued to share how they also needed to work on feeling enough and learning to stop judging and speak more kindly to themselves. Lucy shared with Sylvia how she always compared herself to other mothers now that she was divorced and bringing up her children on her own. I could see Sylvia smiling and embracing the kind words from the shining babes in the group and her energy lifted, even though she found it a little difficult to accept a compliment. She loved the energy of the women– and at the end of the session, she openly said to the group how she wished she could start the day with a SHINE group session, as it was the first time she felt safe to be herself.

Linda's story

Linda, 54, is an assistant school teacher. For most of Linda's life she had suffered from anxiety and lack of confidence. She never felt calm or balanced, and now at this stage of her life, she was starting the menopause, which was having a profound emotional impact in her life. In fact, she had stopped going out and meeting up with her friends as she didn't feel like being out in public or that she had the energy to do anything.

During her third week on my SHINE programme, I asked her if any of her friends were aware of what she was going through and, if so, whether she would be comfortable in sharing how she was feeling. She said no and that she didn't want to bother them, feeling that she didn't think they would understand. I told Linda that, in times when we don't feel like ourselves and are experiencing change within ourselves which may affect our mental wellbeing, it is important to share that with people so we don't feel alone. I asked her to list her friends' strengths and qualities and what values they brought to their friendship, so she could discover which friend to turn to for support with her emotional needs and so that she could form connections.

Linda's squad values and strengths list:

★ **Jenny** – My happiness bringer, someone I am always comfortable with who makes me feel connected and valued

★ **Helen** – My grounder who helps me reflect on myself and what I am grateful for

★ **Kate** – My challenger who always makes me laugh but also makes me question my direction and how I view things

★ **Alex** – My empath, someone I can always turn to for understanding

★ **Kim** – The friend who is most like me and the one I am myself with

★ **Sarah**– My connector, giving me connections to my past and offering happy memories about how we have grown

★ **Lucy** – A newer friend but one I trust, who has shown me support when I needed it and who also understands what I value in life, sharing those values too

When I received Linda's list, I told her that her friends had great qualities and sounded like complete babes who would totally understand, listen and support her. I asked her what she felt she needed right now and who on her list would be able to support her at this moment.

She answered her friend Alex straight away, and from her qualities I could see why.

Before I ended the session, I guided Linda through a visualisation meditation to get her to visualise meeting with her friend and sharing her experience in coping with the new change in her life. What would she say? What did the location look like? How did it feel to share and connect with Alex? When Linda slowly came out of the meditation, she fed back how she felt a huge relief to be able to share her feelings and how she imagined Alex giving a hug of comfort.

Feeling good, I told Linda to set up a date with Alex straight after the session. Later that week, Linda called to tell me how her date went and how wonderful it was to reconnect with her friend, and that both of them had promised to keep in touch with weekly check-ins. She continued by telling me how she had set up a weekend date with her friends Jenny and Helen. She had a new release of energy because she had found safety and trust, but she was also having a lot of fun at the same time. The purpose was to gain Linda's trust and confidence to reach out to the right friend, without her feeling she was burdening them with her problems. It was a mindset that worked in connecting and bonding while they were doing something fun together.

I loved seeing and hearing all these amazing babes just being so open and vulnerable. It was so empowering that we were all the same and dealing with our own battles in our own way, while not feeling alone in the process. When women support other women, there is great empowerment and connection and support. It's the same experience you get when you arrange a catch-up date with your girlfriends and just connect, bond, share stories and have fun! You want more of it. You feel part of a squad that always has your back and that is so badass.

So, how does that sound? A supporting squad that has your back at all times, allowing you to feel that you are not alone, always cheering you on, and nurturing your needs whenever you need it? Reconnecting with friends you have not seen for a while and rekindling a strong relationship that is supportive and fun?

Of course you want that! But, more importantly, you *need* it. Let's get to it now and create a squad that makes you all shine together.

Exercise 5

I get by with a little help from my friends

Step 1: Reflect on your friendships

List down all your friends and when you last saw them. What was the last fun thing you both did together? How did it make you feel? What did you both experience? And why did you stop contacting them? Be honest with yourself: do you want them back in your life?

Step 2: What are your needs from each friendship?

Ask yourself why you are wanting to reconnect with this friendship. What are the values, connection and needs that come with this relationship? Write down each of your friends' names and the values of each one.

Step 3: Identify your friends' strengths

Look at the friendships you are wanting to reconnect, support and build together. What are your friends' strengths? Are they good listeners? Do you have the same interests? Do you like to work out together? Sharing experiences that make you both feel good and connected is a great place to start. When you become more aware of your friends' qualities, it allows you to connect on a meaningful level that you both can enjoy.

Step 4: Reach out and plan in a date

Be brave and contact your friend. Give reasons why you miss them and why you would love to meet up for a catch-up – and then wait and see, with no expectations… If it's a 'hell yes, hun, I've missed you and would love to meet up,' then plan it in and make it fun for you both. But don't be surprised if they have chosen to move on; remember they may have other reasons in their life which mean they cannot make the friendship a priority. The best thing to do is to learn to accept it and move on.

Top tip

Be honest about what your needs are and whether the squad you're creating supports them. Your squad should always feel like it is inspiring you to grow, cheering you on to move forward.

Exercise 6

Yes day weekend with my squad

Step 1: Plan in a wellbeing 'yes day' with your friends

It's time to have fun with your squad and make a weekend of it. Plan in a weekend when you are all available to have fun and connect in feel-good activities.

Step 2: Choose a mood-boosting activity

Each of your friends, including you, picks one activity that will boost your mood– and all of you need to say 'yes' to doing it. For example, it could be a survival boot camp, singing your heart out during a karaoke session, learning to dance salsa or simply having a calm and relaxing spa day. There are no set rules, only that the activity boosts your mood and you all get to connect and have fun! This exercise not only allows you all to come out of your comfort zones but also to connect while having some girl time together.

> ### *Meditation: I support myself and I allow others to support me*

Before we start, set a target as to how you want to feel. Could it be that you want to feel safe, connected, brave and confident, to show up for yourself within your day, or simply feel peace and freedom away from fearful thoughts?

Whatever your intention, set it now quietly to yourself…
Close your eyes and relax, roll your shoulders back and place
your hands with your palms facing up. If you are sitting on
a chair or cross-legged, feel yourself getting grounded, with
your feet connecting to the ground.

Soften your forehead and focus on the rhythm of your
breath going up and down. Feel your lungs fill up with air,
and release it through your mouth.

In this moment there is nothing to do, but you feel safe
and connected to this moment. Now, visualise family and
friends in your squad who bring you joy, love, connection
and support, people who inspire you. Take your time and
visualise each one sitting with you now, holding hands up,
lifting each other and yourself, feeling balanced, calm and
free.

You are so grateful for each and every one of them,
and you embrace each member of your squad with a hug,
gratitude and the joy they bring into your life. You allow all
that love and support in with every breath you breathe in
and out. Continue to allow that loving support in for the
next minute, and I will mind the time.

Now, each member of your squad gives you a final hug
and leaves the circle to continue with their day, leaving you
uplifted and feeling safe in your own presence. You slowly
come back to your body, stretch your arms into the air, catch
a prayer and lower it down to your chest.

Namaste, my darling, and have an amazing day.

To listen to my guided audio meditation, go to the link or scan the QR Code below.

https://www.michelleagbulos.com/meditations

'Bonus resource

Shining Sisterhood membership squad

You can join and sign up for free to my online Shining Sisterhood community on Facebook or through my website at **michelleagbulos.com**. You will have the opportunity to connect, share and meet with other women who have also experienced co-dependent relationships. There are weekly group check-ins, resources and details of upcoming drop in and workshop coaching sessions which you can access while taking the necessary steps to move forward and thrive.

Chapter 9

Embracing My Fabulous Future Self

My story: embracing my authentic self

I remember that night of his arrest. I was in the garden, lighting up my second cigarette while thinking about how the hell I was going to do it on my own. Where was I going to be in five years? I was on maternity leave and I had two weeks to find another home, as I could not continue to pay for the four-bedroom house that we were in. I had no idea how I was going to afford childcare while going back to full-time work. I felt crippled with fear over how I was going to survive out there on my own. With low energy and self-esteem, I felt completely hopeless. Part of me wanted to give up on life, but I was a mother to a six-month-old little girl who needed me more than anything. I had to dig deep in my soul to keep moving forward.

Fast-forward seven years and – with the support of my amazing family and friends, alongside the support of my coach and community – I now live a life that is filled with ease, balance, love and looking at each day with gratitude. Even though I was blessed with a loving squad around me, the true work I needed to do was to work on myself. It was my responsibility to make my mental and physical wellbeing a priority; with the trauma that had built up in me, I needed to be kind and gentle with myself, not feel trapped in a sea of negative emotions. I had to learn to LOVE me again and reconnect to my self-worth, as she was always there, but I had lost my connection with her along the way. I am not going to lie to you – it was not an easy flowing journey to get where I am now. In fact, most of the time I was battling with my old self that had been familiar to me for so long – but by learning to have patience, and with the correct small actions, I could begin to take steps to rediscover who I was and who I wanted to be.

Self-awareness was the key to creating a life that was healthy and inspiring. I needed to look within to work out who I wanted to become and to understand all that I was feeling. It enabled me to notice my habits and behaviour patterns. I reviewed my core values and challenged myself as to whether my behaviour was aligned with them or not. I had to be honest with myself to truly know what I wanted,

"

It was my responsibility
to make my mental and
physical wellbeing a
priority

"

and I had to believe in myself to stand by those values to be able to build up my self-worth. Whenever negative thoughts and old behaviour patterns arose – like speaking badly about myself or thinking I was not worthy of getting what I wanted – I learned to have more self-compassion and not to judge myself for my past mistakes, like realising I had been played by my ex and chose not to see the red flags that were right in front of me, purely because I saw the good in people and loved and trusted my husband. Learning to be more self-aware gave me the confidence to find clarity and comfort in accepting parts of myself I liked or did not like. Understanding why I felt so many different emotions made it easier to manage and cope with them within my day-to-day life and enabled me to choose how I responded to situations that felt challenging.

I made daily efforts to just be present in whatever the day would bring. I started to trust my judgement and became conscious of not overthinking everything, by having faith that whatever I was worrying about would just work out. Most of the time, the things we overthink and worry about never happen, or don't turn out as bad as we feared. The version in our head always seems to look worse.

As the relationship with myself grew, I started creating healthier relationships with others. I was attracting more like-minded people in my life who inspired me to be better and supported my growth. Unexpected opportunities to different avenues in my life opened up before me. I started to believe in me and that I could achieve anything by committing and working hard towards a goal and intention. I am far from the woman who was left betrayed by her bigamist husband. I am confident, embracing life and forever working towards endless self-love. Having done the work on self-awareness and self-compassion laid a path for self-love to enter. I needed to be more compassionate, so that I didn't judge myself or overthink past actions and mistakes. I made this a practice in all areas of my family, work and personal life. Being a coach, I have a responsibility to take care of my own mental wellbeing first, so that I can support others with theirs. So, not only was I embracing a healthier version of me, but it also fulfilled me to help others heal themselves and take the journey towards self-love.

So you see, it's totally possible to embrace that inner fabulous goddess who is wanting to burst out into the world. Let's start to crack open the light that is within you.

What is 'embracing my fabulous future self' about?

In this step, you will start to gain awareness of your old self so that you can begin the journey and get excited about your future self while creating the life you want. You must have awareness of your old self in order to leave that behind and start the journey towards the new you. You will learn to connect to your self-awareness through your breathing and awareness exercises so you can discover and take the necessary steps to move forward towards a goal or intention you want to create in your life.

Why you need to embrace your fabulous future self

★   **You will start your journey to self-love.**

You may not feel like it right now, but you deserve to be loved. However, first you need to start loving yourself. Your journey to self-love is not about getting or arriving there but growing day by day with the core foundations of self-awareness and self-compassion. The process will feel far better than the end goal, and you will learn to move from your old self to a self that is independent, happier, and enjoying life. Once you are embracing the process and showing up for you, you will find that self-love creeps in as a by-product of the fact you are aware, compassionate, and taking small steps towards the future you.

★   **You will start to become more self-aware to what you need to change within yourself.**

It is only when you are fully present with yourself that you can take the right steps and decisions to change. Self-awareness is the core foundation in starting to get to know yourself and witnessing how you behave and react to challenges and situations in your life. We all have self-awareness built into us – it has always been there – but you have not developed the skill to use it to its full potential, especially if you have just come out of a co-dependent relationship and have never made time for yourself to focus on this. When you work at your own pace and focus on one thing, the way you look at things will change, as will the way you think about them, because you become more self-aware about what is happening around you and within your mind and body.

★ **You will feel the benefits and start getting excited about working towards a better you.**

I am telling you now, babes, when you start to feel the benefits of your self-growth, you will feel mega excitement within your whole body. There is nothing more fulfilling than witnessing the change in how you look and how you see and feel about yourself. The love and development of your self-worth will empower you, and you will want more of it. The changes will not happen overnight; it is an ongoing, beautiful process of discovering what you love. You will start to become resilient to daily triggers – things that would have overwhelmed you and made you dwell on them for a day may now, through self-awareness, only last for a couple of hours. You will become the boss of your breath and emotions, and you will feel that you are gaining your power back. That's exactly it! You are powerful, and I am here to remind you of that.

When we make steps forward to become the person we want to be, we create small wins towards endless self-love, and that should be celebrated as part of your healing journey. Healing is like a roller coaster – some days will feel good and motivate you to move forward, and other days will feel uncomfortable, fearful, and like you're going back to the same habits. Remember that this is all part of the process, and working on your mental wellbeing is like exercising a muscle that will get stronger with time.

Let me share with you now a healing win from Bella, a shining babe who is embracing her fabulous future self!

Bella's story

Bella, 46, a teacher and mama, has always struggled to feel enough for herself and others, but she still wanted to strive for more to create a better life for herself and her children. Living in a two-bedroom house with three children was a tight squeeze, and she always felt the financial strain to invest in moving forward while wanting to achieve more. She had experienced toxic behaviour from her ex-partner, who often gaslit her, creating a lack of confidence and a feeling that she could not make it out on her own. The 'not enough' mindset was blocking her from creating the right actions to move forward, because she did not trust her own judgement to make confident decisions.

During our one-to-one session, Bella confessed that she couldn't see her life progressing from where she was at present and was uncertain as to how anything would ever change for her, as she did not believe she was capable of that change. Bella told me that when she was younger, being the only black girl in an all-girl private school, she always questioned her confidence and never spoke up, even though she knew the answers, so she would not be seen as a failure. This was also the same when it came to her relationships.

For Bella to begin to look at herself differently, with more self-love and compassion, I asked her to close her eyes, place her hands on her chest and give herself permission to forgive herself for holding on to the shame she carried and had put upon herself. I then asked her to wrap her arms around herself, like a friend comforting her, and tell herself that she was safe to sit with the feelings she was experiencing. She became teary and upset and, at the end of the visualisation meditation, she said she didn't realise how much pain and self-doubt she had been holding onto and how much pressure she was putting on herself.

Before our session ended, I told her that she had an inner superpower called self-compassion, and it was the key to giving herself the self-love and kindness she deserved. I asked Bella to plan in and commit for the next two weeks to a 'The Future is Now' journal and meditation exercise so that she could apply the steps and find the resources that would allow her to become the woman she wanted to be. This was to motivate Bella with the possibility of 'what if?', giving her a direction to discover by making time to step back, making intentional actions, and not giving up on her end goal.

Planning in 10 minutes of each day to visualise, journal and set her intention gave her steps to gain confidence that encouraged her to see what was possible. She didn't want to see herself in the same place in five years with the same problems, but instead needed to feel inspired to change and want to change. Bella became self-aware of the habits she needed to change, and put her fears and ego aside to make the small steps needed to bring about that change, rather than just continuing to go along with how things were, hoping it would change.

Bella wanted to do what was best for her true self, and planned in time to slow down, make her self-care a priority and have some fun. Job opportunities arose; she applied for a teacher's job with a good salary and working hours that would suit her and her children. She invested in books and resources that would improve her skills and knowledge. Bella gave me regular updates on her progress, and I told her to imagine she already had the job, noting down how it felt; the more she felt it, the more she would attract it. A week after her interview, the school called her to say the job was hers.

With this new approach to visualising a better future, Bella still felt exhausted, but now she was more satisfied that she was creating exciting steps towards her fabulous new self. With this mindset change, she started to see and feel her self-worth, making sure that she was not overdoing it, just naturally co-creating with the universe. Having more faith and hope, and showing up for herself, not only made her feel positive, but also brought benefits that had a positive impact on her family and everyone else she encountered in her life.

Life is what you make of it, babes, and we only have one, so let's make this one the kind where you are always living your best life! Are you ready to prove to yourself that you have what it takes to create the life you fully deserve and want, never settling for anything less than fabulous? I know you are – you have so got this! So, let's start...

Exercise 7

Self-compassion is your superpower

Step 1: Get comfortable in your space

This exercise requires a chair so you can get comfortable in your meditation space. Make sure that you won't be disturbed and, if you're at home, let everyone in your household know that you are taking time out for you. Have a journal and pen ready to note down what comes up for you after the exercise.

Step 2: Start to notice how you feel and be present

Sit comfortably on the chair and keep your feet grounded on the floor. Close your eyes, place one hand on your chest and the other on your stomach, and feel the natural rhythm of your breath going up and down. Now take note of any thoughts that come to mind. Do not judge what comes up; accept it and just be present with it. Take this time to honour it. Take two deep breaths and, when you are ready, open your eyes and write down what came up.

Step 3: Do not judge

What you have written may feel uncomfortable, but you should know that it is safe to feel it and continue to breathe through it. It is very important that you do not judge the thought or yourself, but instead be curious as to why it has come up. When you're ready, gently ask yourself this question: What would you like to be different about the thought? How would you turn it into an action you intend to change?

Here are some examples:

★   Thought – to be more confident in my life. 'I intend to be more confident to make good decisions for myself.'

★   Thought – to stop overthinking and dwelling on things I cannot control. 'I intend to go through my day with ease and know that everything will work out.'

★   Thought – will I be able to heal from my pain? 'I intend to be gentle with myself and I will work at my own pace to heal.'

Now write down your thought and how you intend to turn it into action.

I intend to --

Exercise 8

The future is now

Step 1: 'Visualise your dream life' meditation

Have a journal and pen ready and listen to the guided meditation, embracing your future self. This meditation will guide you to visualise the person you want to be, so you can see and feel your future self.

After the meditation, free flow and write down how it felt to see your future life and self. Who was there? What were you doing? How did you feel about it? Did any specific feelings come up? Note down as much information as you can that came out of your meditation; this will be the inspiration to create it for real.

Meditation: Embracing your future self

Have your journal and pen ready to free flow from your visualisation meditation. Sit in your meditation space, close your eyes and place your hands with palms facing up. Wow, my lovely, truly embrace this time for yourself to congratulate yourself on taking the steps to creating and developing a loving relationship with yourself.

I am proud that you have made yourself a priority, because you matter, and you are an amazing human being. Remember, you are unique and there isn't another person who will experience the life you get to live, and then you live it out as your own.

Connect with your breath now. Get curious, feel deep within, and connect with your heart to the life you truly want.

Imagine five years down the line: what will your life look like? It could be having more space and time in doing more of what you love.

Maybe you could be free from your past and finding love again? It could be starting your own business... Whatever it is, visualise it now.

Where would you be? What is the location? What would you be doing? Are there people, family, friends? What are they wearing? How are other people feeling in your company? Why does this life feel so good? Why does it make you feel so happy and lift your energy?

Sit with this visualisation, and breathe in this moment, embracing how it makes you feel and makes you smile. I will give you two minutes and mind the time... Feel your body soften and relax, feeling at ease within this dream life.

Now, open your eyes and free-write what you have experienced in your meditation. Don't think about it too much; just let your writing flow.

To listen to my guided audio meditation, go to the link or scan the QR Code below.

www.michelleagbulos.com/meditations

Step 2: Reflect and make an intention

Get real and honest with yourself: what small step can you take that will make a change to set you off towards your dream life? This step is to allow time out to connect with your self-awareness to reflect on what one behaviour or habit you could change right now that you can realistically work into your week. Whatever your goal, commit to it, and remember why you have chosen to work towards it.

Step 3: Make the change, and track it

For example, if your intention is to start looking after your body, what step can you create for your body to feel healthier? It might be you waking up earlier three days a week with some gentle stretches, being conscious to drink more water during the day or taking 10 minutes to plan healthier meals. Remember to make your step small at first, because if you make plans to change three habits in one week, it is likely that you will feel overwhelmed with the commitment and give up. To track your progress, download and print my self-love tracker to plan in when to take action, so you can then check it off once it is achieved.

Download planner: **www.michelleagbulos.com/a4planner**

Top tip

Always remember your *why*. Why do you want to make a change? Taking small steps brings about the biggest change. Use my self-love tracker to keep you on track towards becoming your future you, so you can embrace the process. You will feel excited to be working towards it, meaning self-development becomes fulfilling and fun.

Bonus action

Give yourself a meaningful gift. Yes, hun– you get to celebrate your win in just starting to work towards a better you. By just committing to this self-love exercise, you should be so proud of yourself; you're pretty awesome in my eyes. Choose how you would like to celebrate the start of your journey to endless self-love and the life you truly want. Plan in a date with your friends, treat yourself to a night of all your favourite treats, or buy an item you can wear or display that will always remind you that you are starting to make this commitment to yourself. Make the investment in YOU today because, my lovely, you are priceless!

Conclusion

ongratulations! You have done it, babes. You have reached the end of the book, and you should be so proud of yourself for getting this far. There may have been parts of the book that might have triggered you, or given you a little understanding of some of the feelings you have been experiencing in your life, but most importantly you have started to have fun in doing the things you love and making more time for you. Each exercise and step taken within this book has been an opening and opportunity to develop your confidence, rediscover your passions and start to create the dream life you deserve.

By committing to this book, you have learned to:

★ Plan in time to slow down and be present

★ Do more of what you love by putting your needs first

★ Create a network with like-minded women who support each other and never feel that you are alone

★ Make overall wellbeing a priority so that you can work towards a better you.

What are your next steps?

This is just the beginning, my darling. There is so much more you can achieve in discovering your fabulous future self. You have not even scratched the surface of living out your full potential and releasing all that can free you from your past pain. Your healing journey starts right now, here in this moment, so today is the day in creating a life with endless self-love.

Here are some ways you can connect and work with me and support you on your journey to **SHINE.**

★ Join and sign up to my Shining sisterhood community coaching portal through my website: **michelleagbulos.com** and Facebook where you get to connect with me and other amazing women who are developing and supporting each other to grow and heal. You will also find regular updates of up-and-coming themed drop in and challenges online sessions, access to free mindfulness resources and mindful moments from me to start your day on a good note.

★ Sign up to my **SHINE, FLY AND RISE** 12-week self-love mindfulness programme. A bespoke programme where we work together on your co-dependency behaviours, releasing your limiting beliefs and work towards achieving your personal goals to independence. This will include:

3 part mindfulness programme that focuses on the following:

★ **SHINE** – Rediscovering you / **RISE** – Intimacy and creating healthy relationships / **FLY** – Mentorship module to independence and working on your personal goals

★ X 4 online 1:1 coaching session

★ Weekend mindful moments / end of week reflections

★ Mindfulness / meditations / self-awareness exercises / mindful movement

★ Shining sisterhood online group session

Shine Baby Shine

★ Bespoke coaching programme based on my book

★ Weekly 1:1 coaching sessions on the 5 modules of SHINE

★ Free resource pack – Meditations, self-love tracker...

★ X 1 online group session

I would love to hear from you and get your feedback.

★ Please share your wins and feedback on my book and how it has supported your journey. By sharing your wins and experiences, it will greatly empower and inspire other women too – and remember to keep it fun! Tag me and a friend you feel would benefit from my coaching; use the hashtag #shinebabyshine and share your wins through social media platforms below:

★ Facebook: Conscious coach – Michelle Agbulos

★ Instagram: michelle_agbulos

You have got this, babe!

Love, hugs, and endless support,

Michelle xoxo

Thank Yous

To the most beautiful human I know, my daughter Amelia, I am so grateful to be in your life and to be your mama.

My gorgeous family: my Pa, Lola, my sister Jasmine, Sean, Chase and Mason, so blessed and grateful for your loving support. To my inspiring beautiful goddesses and the strongest mamas that I know, Myleene Klass, Alex Anderson, Carryl Thomas, you have always had my back and inspire me every day. To my fun time partner in crime and the best godfather to Millie pops Daniel Clarke, we both love you. To my coach and soul sister Joanna Hunt and Pete Hunt, you both are angels sent to me by the universe. I will always be forever grateful for your loving support in my journey, and inspiring me to write this book. To the beautiful Lindsey Robinson and her team at Brand Fresh for creating my brand to come alive. My work family Sally Anne and the RI crew, always creative and never boring. Your understanding and compassion has always kept me moving forward. To Neil Russell, thank you for your sensitivity and support in making it possible to create a new life for myself and my daughter. To the most wonderful soul Lorraine Murray, thank you for your teaching in meditation so that I was able to rediscover me again.

To my shining clients who shared their beautiful journey in this book – may you all continue to shine. To Ali and Leila and the team at Known Publishing, this has been the most incredible and healing journey for me and giving the opportunity to do it my way. I have LOVED every minute of it!

Printed in Great Britain
by Amazon

19746518R00099